CONTEMPORARY IRISH MORAL DISCOURSE

Contemporary Irish Moral Discourse

ESSAYS IN HONOUR OF PATRICK HANNON

Edited by

Amelia Fleming

the columba press

First published in 2007 by
the columba press
55A Spruce Avenue, Stillorgan Industrial Park,
Blackrock, Co Dublin

Cover by Bill Bolger
Origination by The Columba Press
Printed in Ireland by ColourBooks Ltd, Dublin

ISBN 1 85607 558 3

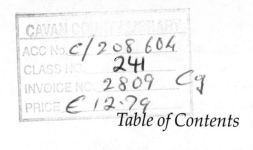

Table of Contents

Acknowledgements

I would like to express my thanks to the contributors for their co-operation with this collection of essays honouring the Rev Professor Patrick Hannon BA (NUI), BD, STL, DD (Maynooth), PhD (Cantab), Barrister-at-Law (King's Inns), Professor/Head of Department of Moral Theology, Maynooth. These essays are intended to be a presentation of the current and future state of Christian moral debate in our contemporary society by some of those Irish moralists who value Patrick Hannon's voice in this discourse.

His professional activities in the field of moral discourse include membership of the Irish Bioethics Council; Advisory Board, Institute of Criminology, Faculty of Law, University College Dublin; Irish Theological Association; Irish Association of Teachers of Moral Theology; British Association of Moral Theology Teachers; European Society for the Study of Theology; and the Canon Law Society of Great Britain and Ireland. He is also on the Editorial Board (formerly editor) of the *Irish Theological Quarterly* and was joint editor of the Maynooth Bicentennial Monographs series.

Among the contributors to this collection are those who have worked alongside Pat in his professional career, and number him among their close friends, and also those of us who have studied under his able supervision. I believe this represents the important influence he has had and will continue to have on how we reflect morally upon our lives, especially those of us who are embarking on our professional lives as teachers in the field. We have had an excellent mentor, and a good friend, and we continue to listen carefully to his voice in our well thumbed copies of *Church, State, Morality and Law*, (Dublin, Gill and Macmillan 1992), *Knowing Right from Wrong*, (Dublin, Veritas, 1995), *Moral Decision Making*, (Dublin, Veritas, 2005), and his recently edited *Moral Theology. A Reader*, (Dublin, Veritas, 2006).

I would also like to express my gratitude to Mr Dermot Gleeson, Barrister and Chairman of Allied Irish Banks PLC, Chairman of the Irish Council for Bioethics, and former Attorney General of Ireland, for his personal and reflective

Foreword to this collection. It is an expression of the widespread affection and respect for Pat. The occasion of his sixty-fifth birthday is a welcome opportunity for us to convey our own gratitude and the gratitude of those, students or otherwise, who may not have had the opportunity to express their sincere appreciation for his encouragement and inspiration to reach our full potential.

Amelia Fleming
Editor

List of Contributors

Hugh Connolly is a priest of Dromore Diocese. He lectures in Moral theology at Maynooth where he is also Vice-President. He has published a book on the Irish Penitentials and one on Sin in the Continuum *New Century Theology* series.

Rev Dr Padraig Corkery is Director of Postgraduate Studies and lecturer in Moral theology at the Pontifical University, Maynooth. He edited, with Dr Fiachra Long, *Theology in the University* and has published in *The Furrow* and the *Irish Theological Quarterly*. His research and teaching interests are in the area of bioethics and Catholic Social Teaching.

Amelia Fleming is a graduate of the Pontifical University, Maynooth, and lectures in theology in the Humanities Department in Carlow College. She has published in *The Furrow, Doctrine & Life*, and the *Irish Theological Quarterly*. Her current research centres on the relationship between Christian faith and contemporary culture.

Raphael Gallagher is an Irish Redemptorist. An Arts Graduate of University College Galway he did his post-graduate theological studies in Rome, Bonn and Paris. Currently he is a visiting Professor at the Alphonsian Academy in Rome.

Dermot Gleeson is a Barrister and Chairman of Allied Irish Banks PLC. He is a former Attorney General of Ireland and previously lectured in Constitutional and Administrative Law, and Jurisprudence. He is Chairman of the Irish Council for Bioethics, and a member of the Board of the Gate Theatre in Dublin. He holds a Primary Degree in Economics and Politics and a Masters Degree in Law.

Donal Harrington taught moral theology for many years in Mater Dei Institute of Education and Holy Cross College, Clonliffe. He is the author of *What is Morality? The Light through Different Windows*.

Linda Hogan is Professor of Ecumenics at the Irish School of Ecumenics, Trinity College Dublin teaching a range of courses including Ethics in International Affairs and The Ethics of Human Rights. She is the author of *Confronting the Truth: Conscience in the Catholic Tradition*, New York, Paulist Press, and London, Darton, Longman & Todd, 2000 and *From Women's Experience to Feminist Theology*, Sheffield, Sheffield Academic Press, 1995, 1998.

Vincent MacNamara SPS is the author of *Faith and Ethics: Recent Roman Catholicism; The Truth in Love: Reflections on Christian Morality*; and *New Life for Old: On Desire and Becoming Human*. He lectures at the Milltown Institute for Theology and Philosophy.

Enda McDonagh is Professor Emeritus of Moral Theology at

Maynooth, and currently Chair of Governing Body of National University, Cork. He is a former President of Irish Association for North-South Relations. Co-author with Stanley Hauerwas of *Appeal to Christians to Abolish War in Twenty-First Century*, his forthcoming book is entitled *Immersed in Mystery*.

Suzanne Mulligan is a graduate of the Pontifical University, Maynooth, and is the Finlay Fellow in Theology at the Milltown Institute, Dublin. She is lecturer in the Department of Moral Theology at Milltown.

Monsignor Denis O'Callaghan, was ordained for the Diocese of Cloyne in 1956, completed Doctorate in Theology (Maynooth) in 1958, appointed Professor of Theology (Maynooth) in 1958, completed Doctorate in Canon Law (Rome) in 1962, and appointed Parish Priest of Mallow in 1982.

Gráinne Treanor is a graduate of the Mater Dei Institute of Education and the Pontifical University, Maynooth. She has taught Religious Education in second level schools and moral theology in the Mater Dei Institute. At the moment she is on leave from her position and is spending her time at home with her two small children, Sorcha and Eoin.

Vincent Twomey SVD was born in Cork 1941, ordained, 1970. Doctoral studies in Theology at the University of Regensburg, Germany. Professor of Dogmatic Theology in PNG and Austria. Currently Professor of Moral Theology at St Patrick's College, Maynooth, Editor, *Irish Theological Quarterly*.

Foreword

Although I have known Pat Hannon for over a quarter of a century, it is a measure of his modesty that it is only when I was asked to write a foreword for this book, that I became aware of the full range of his educational work and his writing. He has always managed to effortlessly bypass every opportunity to draw attention to the extraordinary range of his own intellectual and professional achievements, surely the sign of a fine mind.

Gracious, learned, modest, humourous and kind, he has acted as friend and mentor to a generation of Maynooth graduates, who have found in him a scholarly guide whose understanding extends not just to theology and law, but whose reliable intuitions and insights on matters remote from his professional field could always be relied upon. He has acted as counsellor and advisor to many of his admiring students, not just during their time in Maynooth, but repeatedly as they encountered their own personal and professional dilemmas.

He was never content to confine his insights to the academy, and shared his wisdom with professionals who, on a daily basis, confront and work through moral choices in the course of their work; not just priests but policemen, soldiers, doctors and lawyers.

I have enjoyed the inestimable advantage of his wisdom, his good humour and above all his friendship, for almost three decades.

The range of topics covered by the essays collected here, together with the distinction of their authors, speak eloquently of the esteem in which he is held by a wide group of colleagues and former students, and in themselves comprise a valuable contribution to Christian moral debate at the start of the twenty-first century.

The book is a fitting tribute to his achievements as priest, lawyer, teacher, author and faithful friend. Dr Fleming, who has edited the book, deserves all our thanks.

Dermot Gleeson

CHAPTER ONE

An authentic Celtic voice: The Irish Penitential and contemporary discourse on reconciliation

Hugh Connolly

A recent edition of a leading business newspaper carried a rather striking image on the front page of its commercial section. A photograph depicted the chief executive of a global company together with the CEO of its Japanese arm making a collective bow to the assembled journalists and onlookers as they sought to deliver a fulsome and abject public apology on behalf of their company for its failure to comply with certain Japanese legal and regulatory requirements.[1] Evidently a prior boardroom decision had been taken which recognised that on this occasion and in this cultural setting nothing less than a public display of humility and contrition, as well as the payment of the requisite penalties, would wash with their oriental customer base. Words alone, however sincere, were clearly deemed insufficient.

This little vignette from the world of corporate affairs may seem light years away from the era of the Penitentials. It might nevertheless be reasonably argued that it is but a contemporary representation of the timeless truth – and one which is also to be found at the very core of those medieval manuals of penance – that a purely verbal approach to repentance is neither humanly adequate nor morally sound. The recent proliferation both at home and abroad of tribunals of enquiry, boards of redress and truth and reconciliation commissions seems to point to a deep-seated human desire to have hurts and injustices brought into the light of day in order for a true healing to begin. It points toward a need for stories to be told and rituals to be found for bringing conflicts and conflicting parties into a new space where conflict begins to give way to a more wholesome confrontation of the underlying issue. It is perhaps in this quest for new models of repentance that we can learn from what I would argue is

---

1. *Financial Times*, Tuesday 26 October 2004, 'Citigroup Apologises to Japan', 30.

some remarkably sophisticated philosophy and machinery of reconciliation to be found in the penitential books.

Some years ago, when I was undertaking a doctoral programme with the Gregorian University, I embarked on a study of the Penitentials with a view to unearthing some of the insights of that admittedly primitive era, in order that they might be brought to bear on the contemporary approach to sacramental penance.[2] For me, the era of Irish monasticism which substantially influenced the development of private confession, and which saw the arrival of the Penitential as a new literary genre, was a key moment and one which merited more analysis than had been undertaken to date. Two decades later I have the feeling that some of the observations I then made in the context of individual repentance have a further relevance and application in the contemporary quest for collective expressions of repentance and effective communal models of reconciliation. Further, I believe that the more recent attention to and development of the issue of restorative justice within civil society, and the attendant questions that it poses of a theology of repentance, also warrant a fresh look at these ancient texts.[3]

What happened in the golden age of the Irish church clearly triggered the imagination of people all over the Christian world and beyond. People began to find sustenance and support from a ritual of repentance which had, until then, been severely under-utilised and under-developed. Christian teachings on forgiveness and reconciliation were in that era made present to people in a new and exciting way. Fourteen hundred years later, that excitement has all but disappeared. One suspects that the very terminology of conversion, repentance, penance and the like, seem to carry with them for some people unsavoury resonances of a bygone era. They are seen by not a few to reflect attitudes and practices and an image of God with which the contemporary believer is no longer at ease.

One corrective feature of Irish penance, which I had signalled then as perhaps worthy of attention in this regard, was its 'holistic' dimension. There was a very definite shared conviction

---

2. Published in Connolly, H., *The Irish Penitentials and their challenge for the Sacrament of Penance today*, Four Courts Press, Dublin, 1995.
3. See for instance Marshall, T., *Restorative Justice an Overview*, Home Office Publications, London, 1999 and Van Ness, D., & Heetderks, K., *Restoring Justice*, Anderson Press, Cincinnati, 1997.

among the penitentialists that just as sinful choices are reflected at the physical, mental, emotional and spiritual levels, so too should all of these facets be involved in the curative penitential process. Metanoia could not simply remain a purely intellectual, abstract concept. Instead, once embarked upon, it had to produce real and far-reaching change. Even a preliminary observation of the popularity today of places of real pilgrimage such as Lough Derg, Croagh Patrick, the Camino de Santiago and the like suggests that there remains at least a residue of that holistic approach to penance within the spirituality and religious consciousness of the contemporary Christian.

In that earlier study, I had also argued that part of the problem for the sacrament of penance today arises from the disproportionate emphasis that was given to the canonical dimension. Many people did not feel inclined to celebrate this sacrament because the ritual itself, as they saw it, formed part of an authoritarian world, which they had rejected. Thus, while society, government, the family and Catholic theology throughout the twentieth century had gradually moved away from imperial models and symbols and towards more communitarian expressions of authority, the sacrament of penance was slower to shed its somewhat legalistic and impersonal vocabulary.[4] Although this situation has arguably been addressed at a theological level in both conciliar and post-conciliar documents, it would still seem that fresh thinking at the level of ecclesiology and penitential theology has yet to be mirrored by a corresponding rethink at the level of pastoral praxis. In short, the result was that what should have been an important moment of healing encounter was still marred by an excessive 'mechanism', and more especially by what some commentators have called the 'absolutionist mentality'. That key aspect of confession of sins, which made it a nodal point, along the journey of faith, was somehow neglected and reduced instead to an unhealthy legalism. The result was a tendency toward an excessive verbalism where the penitent merely verbalised all areas of weakness and the confessor, in turn, almost invariably prescribed a verbal act of satisfaction. Ironically part of the reason for the tendency toward verbalism may have been, I believe, a desire to avoid any suggestion that in undertaking a rigorous act of satisfaction, such as those pre-

---

4. For a masterly overview of this see Latourelle. R., *Man and his Problems in the Light of Jesus Christ*, New York, Alba 1982, 375ff.

scribed in the Penitentials, one was somehow earning or merit-
ing divine forgiveness. A simple verbal act of satisfaction could
have no such connotation. Whilst this was no doubt a laudable
aim, the downside was a very real slide into what one might call
a certain 'tokenism'. There was no real sense of challenging
human weakness so as to undo hurts and make good on wrongs
inflicted on others.

For all their severity, the Penitentials had the merit I believe
of avoiding this scenario. They distinguished between 'doing
penance' (*poenitere*) and 'making satisfaction' (*satis facere*). On
one occasion the Penitential of Cummean notes: 'He who utters
in anger harsh but not injurious words shall make satisfaction to
his brother and keep a special fast.' (Cu.IV.13). On the one hand,
there is the imposition of a penance for purposes of correction
and, on the other, there is also a practical prescription to undo
the harm that has been caused. This finds expression in
Cummean's dictum concerning penitents: namely, that after
being led to repentance they are to be (a) corrected of their error,
(b) amended of their vices and (c) rendered such that God is
favourable to them. There is an unexpected refinement and
sense of process and progression here and this is duly reflected
in the prescribed acts of penance.

Likewise there are many instances of acts of satisfaction,
which entail a repayment of what is owed. To be sure these are
often characterised by a juridical tone which, at its worst, tends
to reduce the whole scenario to a logic of commerce and of repayment of debts and dues. The tariff system was, after all, to
become the Achilles' heel of the penitential manuals. However,
even where the emphasis is distinctly flawed, it has the advantage of highlighting tangible deeds that are demonstrative of a
purpose of amendment.

At another level, there is also awareness that wrongdoing
can unleash a whole chain of harmful and damaging consequences that are not simply confined to the perpetrator but can
serve to wreak havoc upon the lives of others. The manual of
Columbanus, reflecting on the situation of a family which becomes destitute because of the killing of the breadwinner, ac-
knowledges that a family would remain destitute if penance
were simply limited to an expression of repentance by the killer.
So it obliges the perpetrator 'to take the place and shoulder the
responsibilities of his victim' (Co.B.13). Similarly in Cummean

in the case of wilful injury the penitentialist sees that the victim's wounds, damages and medical expenses will not be diminished by the mere fact of the aggressor's repentance. The penitent it seems has to be brought to an awareness of his responsibilities. (Cu.IV.9). For the penitentialists, there has to be concrete external evidence of the inner change of heart.

It is clear, then, that they understood the personal and social consequences of sin as not necessarily obliterated by conversion alone. They were convinced that there is a further human and social dimension that goes beyond personal repentance and reconciliation with God. Of course there is no denying that repentance belongs properly to the human heart; but the penitentialists saw it as part of their task, to find creative ways in which conversion could find real expression in daily human activity.

In other words, they proposed an integral, holistic approach to penitential activity. Just as there was a very real and tangible physical dimension to the initial wrongdoing, so too real reconciliation more often than not had to find expression in a material act of reparation. Only in this way, as they saw it, could the person that had been 'infected and wounded' by sin, be integrated, healed and restored via the 'medicine' of penance. Struggle against sin through prayer and ascetic activity was prescribed in plenty, but this ultimately had to spill over into concrete action if repentance were to be complete. For the monastic fathers, (who had a vehement distaste of sorcery and superstitious practices), there could be nothing 'magical' about personal conversion. To be sure, forgiveness was God-given and gratuitous, but the work of overcoming the consequences of sin had to be undertaken and come to fruition in daily life.

I believe that the penitentialists in their own way saw that no system of penance could be built entirely upon a philosophy of retribution, focusing primarily upon punishment and flowing from feelings of revenge. A purely negative philosophy would only produce negative results and the vicious circle of violence would be reinforced. A merely retributive approach, which sought a victory for one or other party, would inevitably fail to get to the truth of a situation. Such a system could not ultimately encourage offenders to take personal responsibility for their actions.

In all this the Penitentials were of course drawing upon a rich tradition. Restoration was the primary focus of biblical justice systems. Despite the widely popular misuse of the concept of *lex talionis*, the law of proportionality, as expressed in the notion 'an eye for an eye,' biblical tradition had a long-standing restorative focus. It was based on the need to seek 'shalom' – the peace and well being of the whole people. Shalom was not simply understood as the absence of conflict. It was construed as peace combined with justice and right relationships. The Law was there to seek, protect and promote shalom. Coupled with shalom was the need to renew and restore the sacred covenant, which the people had with Yahweh. Crime always broke this sacred bond which then needed repairing. As a further need to temper community response, sanctuary became an essential element of justice, as did the special protection of the poor, marginalised, the dispossessed, widows and orphans. The Years of Jubilee, when debts were forgiven, also sought to bring mercy, healing, new life and a fresh start to their processes of justice.

There are, I believe, strong resonances of this biblical approach to repentance in the Penitentials and more particularly in their approach to assigning penances. It was firmly within this theological framework that they made use of Cassian's so-called 'principle of contraries'. According to this approach, each penitent required the undivided, professional attention of the monastic *anamchara* in order that the precise kind of penitential activity would be found to re-orient him or her away from wrongful choices. For this reason, Columbanus recommends that 'spiritual doctors treat with diverse kinds of cures the wounds of souls' and that they 'compound their medicines' after the style of 'doctors of the body'. (Co.B.pr).To the fore here are the diversity and the detail of the acts of satisfaction. These are to be individually tailored according to the individual and to their specific requirements.

In practice, there were several ways in which penances could be thus tailored. Among these were the 'grading' of prescribed penances according to age, health, gender and clerical status. Penances would typically be given using the principle of contraries as a guide and basis for diagnosing the underlying vices and the corresponding virtues. Placed within Cassian's framework acts of penance would become at least theoretically acts of reparation (Cu.pr.l). Despite the oft-repeated criticism that Celtic penance encouraged an unhealthy individualism, the fact remains that those penances, which encouraged the penitent to

make satisfaction to the 'victim', actually enhanced the social
and restorative dimensions of reconciliation. In this respect I believe it was an echo of the collective solidarity that emerged out
of the events of the first Easter and out of God's gesture of
supreme compassion and forgiveness for his people. There, forgiveness had not only a galvanising but also a reparative and
healing or 'making whole' effect. As in the case of Jesus' own
earthly ministry (such as the healing of the paralytic Mk 2:5-12)
forgiveness of sin was clearly linked with healing in the life of
the primitive church. 'Confess your sins to one another' advises
James 'that you may be healed' (James 5:16).

It is this combination of reparative, restorative and re-integ-
rative effects that has come to be described in more contemporary language as *reconciliation*. But the word is often deceptive in
modern usage. Not infrequently it is used to describe the bringing together of warring factions or a new meeting of minds between erstwhile enemies. This is patently not the case in the relationship of God to humanity. While human beings may frequently err and fall short of the goals that they have set themselves, Christian teaching holds that the Father always remains
constant and faithful. It is true of course that the original sense of
the Greek term *katallagé* is of God reconciling all humankind indeed all of the cosmos to himself. Human beings are not 'actively'
involved in this process, instead they are 'granted' reconciliation.
(On this point the Reformers were of course right to insist when
they underscored the assertion that justification is not the result
of human efforts or of the particular merits of the individual but
it is the fruit rather of he who won eternal life for all.) But the
Christian tradition has always had a sense that justification is
achieved and made real by human beings' co-operation with divine grace and that it does not therefore remain purely extrinsic
to the human person. The transformation of the person into the
image of the Son is a co-operative task. It was for this reason that
Jesus opened his public ministry with the clarion call '*metanoieté!*'
'Repent and believe in the good news' (Mk 1:15). The joyful
good tidings of Jesus' kingdom message are therefore an urgent
summons to *metanoia* or a change of heart. The coming of that
kingdom in the person, the life, the ministry and the witness of
Jesus of Nazareth creates an awareness of the absolute need for
God in the human heart. In the gospels, Jesus' life and ministry
are in themselves a call to conversion. They are, for all who en-

counter him, a summons to abandon sin, to turn around, to re-orient their life toward the truth and freedom of the kingdom of God and to restore its reign concretely both in their own life and in the lives of others.

Already too in the prophetic tradition the Hebrew term *shub* had conveyed the sense of a dramatic change of direction as well as a restoration of familial intimacy and a 'returning home' like the return of the prodigal son in Jesus' timeless parable. This meant that conversion was fundamentally about the re-establishment or restoration of the dialogue of love between God and human beings, both individually and in the community. This idea is also captured in the notion of the *ruah* Yahweh in Ezekiel, which breathes new life into what have become 'dry bones'. The dry bones afflicted by the desiccation of sin are in consequence revitalised and raised to new life. The 'change of heart', which the prophets and the psalmists unceasingly call for, is that kind of dramatic event which although rooted in personal conversion is ultimately restorative not only of the individual but of an entire community.

It is of course true that the penitentialists did not exploit to its full potential the restorative dimension of their theology of 'cure by contraries' and too often resorted to the more easily weighted and calculated days, weeks or even years of fasting. But this penance did, at least in theory, aim at a rehabilitation of the whole person and at undoing the more far-reaching effects of sin both individual and collective. In this regard the preponderance of medicinal language is also instructive. Columbanus portrays the *anamchara* as a 'spiritual doctor' who enables cure to take place. Similarly, Cummean's text is so replete with this imagery that it styles itself as a treatise on the 'remedies of wounds' and it is only later that one discovers that these 'wounds' are moral rather than physical. Even the so-called Bigotian text, which is perhaps more given than others to the language of judgement and retribution, reminds its readers that confessors are 'healers of souls' and as such they will necessarily pay great attention to age, sex, moral strength, instruction and personal disposition before deciding upon a penance. And likewise there is a reminder that the soul-friend's final decision must be reasonable; given neither to an undue leniency, on the one hand, nor to a disproportionate severity, on the other. 'Wise men in regulating penance are to look carefully also to this, not to punish with the rod a crime worthy of the sword nor to smite with the sword a sin worthy of the rod.' (Bl.pr.3)

The essence of the good penance then for the penitential authors is that it be, at once, both salutary and suitable. One should not act arbitrarily when assigning penances but instead make a prudent and just decision. The good penance, after all, is to be but an incarnation of the principle of contraries. In other words, any interior change of heart has to find real and meaningful expression in external attitudes and actions. And so, in and through the importance that they attach to the metaphor of healing and of the 'principle of contraries', the penitentialists very clearly seek to shift the focus on to the reparative and restorative dimensions of repentance.

Of course one cannot get away from the fact that, Irish penitential theory and practice is very much part of an ascetic tradition. Building upon the tradition of the Desert Fathers and drawing also upon the indigenous, predecessor culture, it laid down very rigorous penitential prescriptions and, as we have already noted, too often honoured the principle of contraries in theory rather than practice. Prayer, fasting and almsgiving gradually became the preferred acts of penance and gained near universal dominance. But looked at in another way, these might be described as the traditional 'staples' of a regime, which nonetheless aimed at a holistic programme of repentance and recovery. Fasting demonstrated sincerity of purpose, prayer adherence and attachment to Christ and almsgiving and charitable works underlined the restorative dimension. In the Penitentials there could be no dichotomy between conversion of heart and conversion of life. In other words, asceticism was not to be construed as an alternative to restorative justice but as an important ally and aid. Prayer and fasting in this scheme of things would become the penitential grammar of a new moral life on to which the penitentialists would graft the various other-centred exercises depending on the exigencies of the particular situation.

In a very real sense this form of asceticism and penitential discipline looked forward rather than backward. Throughout the penitential literature there is a constant striving and searching for the equilibrium between undoing harm and renewing commitment. A case in point is the Old Irish text which states that the aim of the penitential is for 'annulling and remedying'. It is never simply a question of 'wiping the slate clean' by removing or annulling the negative element. There has also to be a parallel process, of engagement or re-engagement with the moral life. (Co.Inst.X. Cf Gal 2:20)

The penitent who engaged in ascetic practices was not demonstrating what 'they could do' for God, but was instead recalling the gospel imperative to go and make peace with one's brother before being reconciled at the altar. This attitude to forgiveness and reconciliation, far from being an impoverishing one, served I believe to enrich, liberate and render life more heroic. It was a way of looking at things more honestly and realistically and of not getting enmeshed with false 'securities'. To the protagonists of Irish monasticism penance would have lost all meaning were it simply used as a charm, either to escape reality or else merely to fulfil the terms of a punishment. Instead, it had to be truly re-orienting and genuinely restorative.

A final two facets of the Penitentials susceptible to making a contribution to the contemporary debate on reconciliation are their insistence on candour and honesty, on the one hand, and genuine readiness to change, on the other. For the monastic fathers honesty, truth and a willingness to acknowledge the reality of failure are pre-requisites on the path to *metanoia*. They are also of course a *sine qua non* for contemporary recovery programmes and conflict resolution scenarios. A decisive moment of acceptance of reality and of the need for assistance from without is essential. Recovery entails a commitment to the truth and to an attitude of honesty. The church as a community of believers has a responsibility to provide the dynamic context of faith, hope and love where all are given the opportunity to begin and nourish their individual and collective recovery from sin.

Truthfulness and openness are thus starting points for both the individual and collective processes of reconciliation. For this reason rituals that gloss over, or somehow fail to get to grips with, a real and integral admission of guilt are of dubious value, and indeed may even be counterproductive insofar as they cheapen and trivialise what should be a profound and meaningful moment. For this reason too, I think we have begun to rediscover ways in which repentance can take place within the setting of the community at prayer. These rituals tend to underline our belief that the way in which we seek reconciliation with God is in and through reconciliation with his others. But the essential components of personal honesty and disclosure remain. It is only in naming and owning fault that conversion becomes real. For the penitentialists the moment of confession and conversion was a very profound time of healing and it could no more be adequately fulfilled by a vague or generalised expression of remorse than a physical cure from illness could be effected by a superficial or incomplete medical examination.

In analogous ways, perhaps communities, societies and cultures also need to make a decisive break with the sinful past in order to recover collectively from the poisonous effects of sin. In mid 1990s South Africa, for instance, the collapse of apartheid left behind a legacy of distrust and hurt. By way of a remedy the old National Party favoured a Reconciliation Commission, whereas the African National Congress (ANC) sought nothing less than a painstaking investigation of the truth. The resultant comprise, the Truth and Reconciliation Commission, although not entirely unflawed, provided a much needed cathartic process and in its very name gave expression to a basic pre-requisite for the healing of collective hurt. Confession, admission and acknowledgement of responsibility and ultimately of sin are necessary purgatives, purifying and ultimately healing acts whether an individual or an entire community undertakes them.

A second condition in the penitential literature is some kind of interior readiness for moral renewal. In classical theological language this might have been described as a 'firm purpose of amendment'. What was meant here was a realisation that conversion entailed personal and, on occasion, collective effort to overcome the effects of evil, whether from within or from without. No penitent in the Irish monastic discipline could have been in any doubt that what was being demanded of them was genuine physical commitment and engagement. Of course, at a purely theological level, the wholly gratuitous nature of God's pardon was unquestioned. But there was also a clear recognition that human beings do not experience themselves solely at a spiritual level. Accounts of Jesus' ministry in the gospels frequently attest to the same insight. In one well known episode a paralytic's friends are asked by Jesus 'Which is easier to do – to say to this man your sins are forgiven or to say get up take up your bed and go home?' Clearly the first option is the easier since forgiveness is not readily susceptible to external verification. The episode ends, however, with Jesus summoning the sick man to his feet and his mobility being thus restored. Morally the paralytic had already been healed by the Jesus' words of forgiveness; humanly it became much easier to accept this when it found a resonance in his physical cure.

Grace of course can never be purchased, forgiveness cannot be earned but neither can we ignore the serious duty of reparation, the need to reconstruct our lives and the obligation to undo the hurt and the harm we have visited on others. There is an inescapable logic in that sin, and those effects of sin that are primarily physical in expression, should be countered in a physical and tangible way. For en-fleshed human beings it makes sense that the entire human person, body, mind and spirit should be somehow engaged in the process of conversion and reparation for the wrong which has been done. The biblical example of Zaccheus is instructive here: 'Behold, Lord, the half of my goods I give to the poor; and if I have defrauded anyone of anything, I restore it fourfold' (Lk 19:8). The Penitentials' adoption of the traditional forms of penance in prayer, fasting and almsgiving gives expression to ancient ecclesial wisdom, which directed penance toward outreach, concern, and support for others.

A recent article in a South American religious journal speaks of the danger of contemporary Chileans becoming 'orphans of memory', since collectively as a nation they have failed to come to a shared remembering of the 1973 *coup d'état* and its aftermath.[5] The danger is that society would simply acquiesce into an uneasy peace built upon collective amnesia in the hope that somehow deep wounds and societal divisions might somehow disappear. But the near universal experience of conflict resolution projects is that true healing just cannot be achieved in this way. Geiko Muller-Fahrenholz, a German Lutheran theologian who has written compellingly on the holocaust and the lessons it holds for us suggests, that there is much more wisdom in the Jewish proverb 'Forgotten prolongs captivity. Remembering is the secret of redemption,' than in the popular, adage 'forgive and forget'. He speaks of the 're-membering' in the sense of bringing together the members and pieces of something that was once complete; a restoration of what has been lost and a joining together of what had been broken.[6] Remembering for him is therefore a process, which calls to mind the deepest con-

5. Hurtado, P., ¿Huérfanos de Memoria? *Mensaje*, Vol 52, Santiago Chile, September, 2003, 30-34.
6. Muller-Fahrenholz, G., *The Art of Forgiveness*, WCC Publications, Geneva, 1996, 122ff.

victions and possibilities of people, encourages them to heal forms of dismemberment and to work toward a better more integrated society. Confession, admission and acknowledgement of responsibility and ultimately of sin are therefore necessary purgative, purifying and ultimately healing acts, but humanly the process is incomplete until they spill over into restorative and reparative action. It is my belief that the Penitentials, for all their severity, not only championed the confession of fault as a profoundly healing and necessary experience but did so in a way which sought to re-member, in the aforementioned sense of reintegrating what is broken and fragmented. It has been suggested that an unfortunate effect of Christianity aligning itself with Roman law was that it essentially became a proponent of punishment and retribution and lost sight of the rich biblical restorative tradition.[7] Whatever the validity of that critique, it would seem fair to say that a disproportionate emphasis on absolution has been to the detriment of the notions of satisfaction and amendment, and perhaps left our rituals of repentance themselves open to the charge of acquiescing in amnesia.

The time would therefore seem ripe for a rediscovery of the restorative dimension in these rituals in a manner that addresses both individual and collective needs. It is my belief that this quest can profit from the inspiration and insight of the Penitentials, which proved to be such a formative influence in our tradition. Like those western executives in Japan who saw the need to give physical expression to their contrite and repentant state, perhaps the time has come to nudge our rituals beyond verbal and token expressions and toward concrete acts of reconciliation and restoration.

---

7. Hadley, M., *The Spiritual Roots of Restorative Justice*, New York University Press, Albany, 2001, chapter 3.

CHAPTER TWO

Bio-ethics and
contemporary Irish moral discourse

Padraig Corkery

Since the birth of Louise Brown in 1978 there has been much discussion worldwide on the ethics of reproductive technologies. Professional ethicists and the public at large have addressed significant questions concerning the nature of human parenthood, the status of human life at its earliest stage of development and the role of science in the area of human reproduction.[1] Societies have, in general, argued that reproductive technologies have societal consequences and should therefore be regulated by society through the civil law. Many societies set up interdisciplinary groups to assist in the forming of legislation in this area. The commission set up under the leadership of Dame Warnock in Britain is probably the best known example of the work of such a group and their influence on the formation of legislation.

The fundamental issues raised by reproductive technologies have generated much debate and disagreement. There is no unanimity on ethical questions concerning the status of the pre-implanted embryo or on the nature and scope of human parenthood. This debate is well-documented in the journals and textbooks of bioethics over the past twenty five years. It is no surprise, therefore, that the regulation governing the practice of IVF and other reproductive technologies differ significantly from society to society. The shape and content of legislation in this area flows naturally from a society's response to the core ethical issues.

The response of the Catholic tradition to IVF and other reproductive technologies is clearly set out in *Donum Vitae* published in 1987. A central argument of this document is: 'What is technically possible is not for that very reason morally admissible.'[2] As moral agents responsible for our actions we are called to exam-

---

1. Part of this article was first published in *The Furrow* 56 (June 2005): 353-7. Used with permission.
2. *Donum Vitae*, Introduction, Section 4.

ine the means used to achieve the undeniable good that is the birth of a child. After a systematic examination of the process of IVF, rather than just the consequences, reproductive technologies were rejected as incompatible with a Christian anthropology and a Christian understanding of responsible human stewardship. In particular the practice of freezing, discarding and experimenting on 'surplus' embryos was rejected as incompatible with the respect due to the embryo. Catholic tradition claims that the embryo is a part of the human family and should 'be respected and treated as a person from the moment of conception'.[3] Furthermore the process of IVF was deemed to be inattentive to our nature as embodied persons called to procreate through bodily union in the context of marriage. The introduction of third parties, either as donors of genetic material or as surrogates, was seen to be counter to the Christian vision of marriage and the family as the locus for the procreating of children. Finally, *Donum Vitae* raised important questions about the language of 'a right to have a child' and its possible negative impact on children and their dignity.[4]

Ireland and IVF

Irish society is quite unique in how it has responded to date to the question of regulating IVF. Unlike most countries there is no legislation here governing this area of life. Instead the Codes of Conduct of the Irish Medical Council and the Irish Institute of Obstetricians and Gynaecologists have provided the only guidelines in this area. Over the years these have evolved reflecting changing attitudes to certain aspects of reproductive technologies. Earlier versions, for example, restricted IVF to married couples and excluded the donation of gametes. The most recent Guidelines make IVF more readily available and allow for donation of both gametes and embryos.[5] The absence of legislation in this area was perceived by most commentators to be unsatisfactory. In response to this unease and to directives from the EU the former Minister of Health Micheal Martin set up the

---

3. Ibid., Chapter 1, Question 1.
4. Ibid., Chapter 2, Question 8. 'A true and proper right to a child would be contrary to the child's dignity and nature. The child is not an object to which one has a right ...'
5. The Medical Council, *A Guide to Ethical Conduct and Behaviour*, (Sixth Edition), 2004. Section F.

Commission on Assisted Human Reproduction in March 2000. The brief of the Commission was to 'prepare a report on the possible approaches to the regulation of all aspects of assisted human reproduction and the social, ethical and legal factors to be taken into account in determining public policy in this area.' As part of the process the Commission organised a public conference in February 2003.[6] Two years later their long awaited Report was published and presented to the Government for their consideration.[7] After deliberating on the Report, the Government is expected to introduce legislation to govern this important and expanding area of contemporary medicine.

The publication of this Report should generate debate within Irish society on the possible shape of legislation in this sensitive and important area of life. The possible shape, content and tone of the debate might tentatively be sketched from the discussion among Irish contributors, including Professor Patrick Hannon, over the past twenty years. Though the discussion was never very robust, a review of some of the important texts reveals key questions, areas of disagreement and tensions. In the remaining pages of this essay I will identify the key concerns and propose some guidelines that might enable any future Irish debate on reproductive technologies to be enlightening, intellectually robust and moderate in tone. It is to be hoped that a debate on the content of legislation, in an increasing pluralistic society like Ireland, will be a 'learning experience' for all.

Soon after its publication, *Donum Vitae* was reflected on by Patrick Hannon. He correctly predicted that professional theologians would continue to seek 'a more cogent demonstration of the universal wrongness of conception by IVF and ET'.[8] He also raised the question of the status of the Instruction and its binding force. He judged that the Instruction was somewhat below and encyclical in status but still represented an exercise in authoritative magisterium. Given the reality of disagreement on the conclusion of the instruction he argued for the primacy of in-

---

6. www.cahr.ie
7. *Report of the Commission on Assisted Human Reproduction*, April 2005. The text is available on the Department of Health and Children website: www.dohc.ie/
8. Patrick Hannon, 'In Vitro Fertilization', *The Furrow* 38 [1987]: 739-746. See also *The Furrow* 39 [1988]: 121 for Hannon's response to correspondence generated by his original article.

dividual conscience for those who had a 'bona fide inability to see the binding force of the Instruction's teaching.'[9]

In a later expanded version of this article, Hannon again raised concerns about the Instruction's central argument re the inseparability of the unitive and procreative dimensions of human sexual intercourse.[10] This argument was developed at length in *Humanae Vitae* but Hannon questioned its applicability in the context of IVF and ET.[11] Secondly he judged that the arguments presented in the Instruction against extra corporeal fertilisation seemed 'tendentious'.[12] Finally, he again raised a question about the status of the Instruction and indicated a positive role for individual conscience once the traditional norms governing the formation of conscience are observed.

The Irish bishops and reproductive technologies
Not surprisingly the Irish Catholic Bishops have consistently provided a moral analysis of developments in the area of reproductive technologies. In an early intervention they raised two central objections to IVF.[13] Their primary argument centred on the destruction of the embryo and the use of the embryo as a means to an end. Underpinning this argument was the understanding that embryonic life is entitled to respect and protection from the moment of fertilisation. Their second argument rested on their claim that through IVF the generation of life becomes a technical process, controlled by experts, and ultimately 'becomes dehumanised'.[14] It is worth noting that they made no explicit mention of the 'separation of ends' argument which was to feature centrally in *Donum Vitae*. Finally, they argued both for greater education about and research into the causes of infertility.

Recently a much more detailed analysis was published by the Bishops.[15] Three principles were identified as central to a

9. Ibid., 746
10. Patrick Hannon, 'In Vitro Fertilization', *ITQ* 55 [1989]: 7-17.
11. Ibid., 14-5, 'An analogy with the case of IVF and ET cannot be pressed.'
12. Ibid., 15
13. Irish Catholic Bishops Commission for Doctrine, 'In Vitro Fertilization', *The Furrow* 37 [1986]: 197-200.
14. Ibid., 199
15. Bishops' Committee on Bioethics, *Assisted Human Reproduction: Facts and Ethical Issues*, Dublin, Veritas, 2000. A second edition of this text was published in April 2003. This slightly revised text can be found at www.catholiccommunications.ie/pastlet/ahr.html

proper evaluation of developments in reproductive technologies: the right to life and bodily integrity; the right to an identity
of origin; the essential meaning of human sexuality. What is immediately striking about this document compared to *Donum
Vitae* is its language and tone. This is seen strikingly in its omission of any reference to the language of 'product' to describe the
fruit of IVF, which featured in the earlier document of the
Congregation, and in its inclusion of a short section on conscience. The treatment of conscience is gentle and identifies religious faith as 'an important element' in the process of conscience
formation. Further it unambiguously advocates that 'each individual must make and be guided by a judgement of conscience.'[16]
Moderate language is also seen in its reflection on the role of
technology in the intimate area of procreation: 'Technology,
often unawares, introduces into the act of life-giving elements
that do not sit well with the dignity of the human person.'[17] At a
later stage the document concludes with a question rather than
an outright condemnation: 'We must question whether such a
highly technological process is a suitable vehicle for the love and
the mystery which, properly speaking, is so central to the generation of a human person.'[18]

In its ethical evaluation of IVF the primary argument used is
that the process is destructive of the embryo. Such destruction, it
argues, is an intrinsic dimension of such technology; '– it is very
difficult to provide IVF effectively without going down a path
that inevitably leads to the death of a great proportion of human
embryos.'[19] Furthermore the Bishops argued that, though destructive research on embryos is prohibited in Ireland, IVF prac-
tised there is 'dependent on research done elsewhere'.[20]
Implicitly the document raises the question of co-operation in
the wrongdoing of others. The use of multiple embryos, the disposal of surplus embryos or their storage is evaluated negatively
because such actions contribute to an ethos that sees the embryo
as a means to an end rather than and end in itself.

The document contains a four-line summary-style ethical
evaluation of IVF that includes: '[i]n many cases it is inconsistent

---

16. www.catholiccommunications.ie/pastlet/ahr.html Chapter 1.
17. Ibid.
18. Ibid., Chapter 3, Section B.
19. Ibid.
20. Ibid.

with respect for the family and the identity of origin of the child. With regard to the integrity of human sexuality, IVF is, to say the least, intrusive.'[21] The language used here is strangely imprecise in a document setting out the moral stance of the Catholic community. It could leave the reader with several questions and some uncertainty. Does intrusive mean morally unacceptable? Could such intrusion ever be justified? Later in its evaluation of GIFT, the document employs language that similarly lacks clarity: 'It does replace the act of intercourse, rather than assisting it, but it is arguably less intrusive in terms of the integrity of sexuality, because it does not totally remove the element of mystery and the randomness of natural fertilisation.'[22] This imprecision in language is repeated in the documents evaluation of AIH and IUI: 'Strictly speaking, AIH and IUI do not respect the integrity of the sexual act, although relative to other procedures the level of intrusiveness is minimal.'[23]

While the absence of legislation in the area of assisted human reproduction is judged to be unsatisfactory, the document does not offer any proposal on the possible shape of legislation. Furthermore, the document does not oppose the allocation of public funding for procedures like IVF but insists on the need to establish 'just and reasonable' criteria for the selection of candidates.[24]

Other Irish voices
This absence of legislation in this area meant that the only guidelines on ethical practice were those set out by the medical profession. These guidelines have been revised several times in the past twenty years and the resulting changes provide an indication of the quiet evolution of the debate in Irish society. The Institute of Obstetricians and Gynaecologists first addressed the ethical issues surrounding IVF in the early 1980s. These initial guidelines were quite restrictive in several respects. They limited

---

21. Ibid.
22. Ibid., 32. The first edition of the document reached a definitive judgement on this issue: 'it does however, replace the act of intercourse, rather than assisting it, and for that reason is *not* morally accepted.' Emphasis mine.
23. Ibid.
24. Ibid., Chapter 4, Section 2. It mentions in particular marital status and age.

the availability of IVF to married couples and insisted that all embryos were to be replaced in the potential mother's uterus. The production or storage of embryos for research purposes was explicitly prohibited, as was third party donation of genetic material.

The 1992 guidelines of the Institute reflected a slight change with regard to the availability of IVF; the original constituency of married couples was broadened to couples. It is interesting to note, however, that the Medical Council retained the original wording in their *Guide to Ethical Conduct*. The guidelines again demanded that all embryos be replaced and added that 'optimally this should be three in any treatment cycle.'[25] The guidelines on IVF in the sixth edition of the Medical Council (2004)[26] again prohibit the creation of life for experimental purposes and the deliberate destruction of the fertilised ovum. These guidelines for the first time allow for the donation of fertilised ova to a third party.

The Guidelines published over the past twenty years governing the conduct of the medical profession contain both elements of change and consistency. There has been a clear change in the constituency that can avail of IVF and in the rules governing third party involvement as donors and recipients of gametes and fertilised ova. There has been a change also in nomenclature from embryo to fertilised ova. The guidelines have been consistent in their prohibiting of the deliberate destruction of the embryo and of the creation of the embryo for experimental purposes.

Donal Murray[27] has made an important contribution to the ongoing conversation in Irish society. In an early work he focused primarily on the nature of ethics and how we decide 'the good'. Experience reveals that people approach the project of 'doing ethics' quite differently and this often results in a pluralism of conclusions on specific issues. Murray, working out of the Catholic moral tradition, argues that the human act in its entirety must be looked at for a proper ethical analysis rather than just consequences or motives. He reflects on IVF in light of the 'truth

25. Medical Council, *A Guide to Ethical Conduct and Behaviour*, appendix G, 62-63.
26. Medical Council, *A Guide to Ethical Conduct and Behaviour* (Sixth Edition 2004) Section F.
27. Donal Murray, *A Question of Morality: Christian Morality and In Vitro Fertilisation*, Veritas, 1985

about human persons and relationships' and identified three dimensions of reproductive technologies that contradict this truth. The first revolves around the process itself; it is by its very nature controlled and views the child as a 'product'. His second objection focuses on the 'quality control' dimension of reproductive technologies. This feature results in the discarding of 'imperfect' embryos and reveals an understanding of human dignity that runs counter to that proposed by the Christian tradition. In that tradition our dignity as persons is intrinsic; it flows readily and universally from our nature as sons and daughters of God. Such a vision explicitly rejects an understanding that links dignity to health, utility or indeed virtue. Finally, using the well-utilised 'slippery slope' argument, he predicted that the 'simple case' of IVF would inevitably lead on to other developments that raise even greater ethical concerns.[28]

In a later contribution[29] Murray again returns to the reality of disagreement on what constitutes morality. This disagreement results in people of 'good will' engaging in bitter arguments on the morality of specific issues. In highlighting this reality Murray has made an important contribution; in contemporary debate about stem cells or the like there appears underlying disagreement about how 'to do ethics'. Do good consequences yield a 'good' act? Are good motives sufficient? Is individual fulfilment and happiness an adequate measure of morality? Besides identifying this root cause of much moral disagreement Murray raised another important concern. Because of the rapid pace of scientific advance and the secretive nature of much research, moral reflection on new developments often happens 'post event'.[30] Because of this delay in moral reflection the contribution of ethicists is often seen as interfering and negative. Ideally, ethicists should be involved at the earliest stage of research rather than presented with a *fait accompli*.

Another earlier commentary came from Kevin Doran.[31] This work closely mirrors the arguments presented in *Donum Vitae*, especially its argument on the status of the embryo. Doran iden-

---

28. Ibid., 22-3.
29. Idem, *The Doctors' Dilemmas: Moral and Ethical Problems of In Vitro Fertilisation*, Veritas, 1988.
30. Ibid., 7-8
31. Kevin Doran, *The Wanted Child and In-Vitro Fertilisation*, Veritas, 1987.

tifies the primary question as: 'Does it [IVF] look on people as having value in themselves, or does it see people as disposable?'[32] A refreshingly broader perspective is found in a recent publication by philosopher Dolores Dooley. She looks at the ethical issues surround NRT from the perspective of a balance between individual liberty and the demands of the common good.[33] She ponders whether the widespread availability of NRT might make the following vulnerable: 'people with impairments, the economically marginalized, women and parents.'[34] She raises the question whether the availability of pre implantation genetic detection creates and promotes societal attitudes against the disabled? Does it shape societal attitudes towards the childless?

The Commission on Assisted Human Reproduction
The Commission on Assisted Human Reproduction[35] held a one-day conference in February 2003. The papers presented there, and more particularly the exchanges from the conference floor, revealed disagreement on a range of issues and an almost complete lack of engagement between the different perspectives. The exchanges were passionate but sometimes revealed intolerance.

Baroness Warnock, in the opening address to the conference, immediately identified the status of the early embryo as the fundamental and irresolvable source of moral disagreement. The best that could be hope for, she argued, was that people who hold different views on that core issue could reach agreement in the framing of regulations that would meet with general approval. She also strongly argued for Government regulation of all aspects of assisted human reproduction rather than allowing market forces to dictate the pace. Though she accepted the reality of the legal prohibition on reproductive cloning, she saw many benefits to the practice of therapeutic cloning: the creation and destruction of a cloned embryo in order, for example, to

32. Ibid., 12. Emphasis added.
33. Dolores Dooley, 'Moral Free-Fall in Ethics: Rethinking Reproductive Responsibility' in Dolores Dooley et al, *Ethics of New Reproductive Technologies: Cases and Questions*, Berghahn Books, Oxford, 2003, 71-5.
34. Ibid., 172.
35. Commission on Human Reproduction: Public Conference, www.cahr.ie

acquire new knowledge. She argued that moral pluralism on these issues within Europe and within countries is to be expected. As she concluded her paper she made two assertions that are worth noting. The first was that the stance of those who see the destruction of the embryo as immoral is 'almost always derived from religion.'[36] The accuracy and, indeed, relevance of this claim needs to be questioned. Though many do base their arguments against embryo destruction on a religiously inspired anthropology and worldview, there are also those who reach the same conclusion working out of a humanist or secular worldview. Her second comment was that the 'law in European society will and should be based on a secular consensus.'[37] It is difficult to discern exactly what she meant by that comment. Did she mean that those who engage life from a religiously motivated worldview are excluded from contributing to societal debate? If so, this claim certainly needs to be challenged. Common sense reveals to us that everyone works out of a worldview that gives them an understanding of themselves and the world they inhabit. In a very real sense, reason works within this framework of understanding. A secular framework is as much a framework as a religiously motivated vision about life and its meaning. Both understandings inform and shape the exercise of reason. Both direct the person in the ordering of priorities and values. It is also obvious that neither way of understanding the world can be proved or disproved. To claim that a secular mind-frame is more 'objective' and, therefore, the only legitimate participant in public debate is both disingenuous and destructive of society. Both worldviews, and the reasoned argument they generate, are legitimate in the public domain.

In another of the conference papers Brendan Purcell presented a very different approach.[38] He engaged the question under three headings: ontological, ethical and legal and argued for the protection of the embryo using a continuity argument. He strongly urged the Commission to see the humanity of the embryo as a member of a 'vulnerable group'.

In its Report the Commission made over forty recommendations governing the whole area of the regulation of assisted

---

36. Ibid., 8
37. Ibid.
38. Brendan Purcell, www.cahr.ie, Session 2, 1- 4.

human reproduction.[39] Some of these are quite controversial and radical in their scope and are certain to be the focus of energetic debate in the months ahead. The more controversial ones involve the nature of human parenthood and the treatment of human life in the earliest stage of development. The following recommendations are particularly challenging, both from the perspective of ethics in general and from the perspective of the anthropology and world vision of *Donum Vitae*.

No 10: 'Appropriate guidelines should be put in place by the regulatory body to govern the options available for excess frozen embryos. These would include voluntary donation of excess healthy embryos to other recipients, voluntary donation for research or allowing them to perish.'[40]

No 16: 'The embryo formed by IVF should not attract legal protection until placed in the human body, at which stage it should attract the same level of protection as the embryo formed *in vivo*.'[41]

No 30: 'Surrogacy should be permitted and should be subject to regulation by the regulatory body.'[42]

No 34: 'Embryo research, including embryonic stem cell research, for specific purposes only and under stringently controlled conditions, should be permitted on surplus embryos that are donated specifically for research. This should be permitted up to fourteen days after fertilisation.'[43]

No 36: 'Regenerative [therapeutic cloning] medicine should be permitted under regulation.'[44]

No 40: 'Pre-implantation genetic diagnosis (PGD) should be allowed, under regulation, to reduce the risk of serious genetic disorders. PGD should also be allowed for tissue typing only for serious diseases that cannot otherwise be treated.'[45]

The future debate
The literature reviewed here, and indeed most of the literature

---

39. *Report of the Commission on Assisted Human Reproduction*, April 2005. The text is available on the Department of Health and Children website: www.dohc.ie
40. Ibid., xv
41. Ibid., xvi
42. Ibid., xvii
43. Ibid.
44. Ibid., xviii
45. Ibid.

generated by Irish theologians and philosophers,[46] has focused on the status of the embryo as a central concern. To a lesser extent contributors have examined the nature of ethics. In the year ahead, these will also be central to the ongoing discussion. Indeed the latter question is one that could be profitably aired and developed in a public debate. How do we as individuals and society evaluate human actions? Is there a consistency in our approach? Are we utilitarian in some areas of life (stem cell research) and advocates of a Christian moral stance in other areas (torture of suspected terrorists)?

As important as these substantive issues are, there are also important questions about the tone and conduct of the future debate. If the bitterness and non-engagement of previous debates on the content of legislation in Ireland is to be avoided, there is a need for some clear ground rules. In this regard a contribution by Richard McCormick,[47] during the abortion debate in America, provides ten useful pointers that may enable the future debate to be conducted in a manner that enables dialogue. Hannon,[48] in an article reflecting on the child abuse scandals in Ireland, has already creatively engaged with this article. In the original article McCormick included the following in his list of rules: try to identify the core issues at stake; represent the opposing position accurately and fairly; avoid the use of slogans; and distinguish morality from public policy. Adherence to these rules by participants may result in a debate that is robust, informative but free from hysteria.

McCormick's last 'rule', and the distinctions underpinning it, have been addressed in depth by Hannon in his work on church and state.[49] It has also been addressed in previous Irish debates on contraception, abortion and divorce but has not been seriously

---

46. Other important works include; Teresa Iglesias, *The Dignity of the Individual: Issues of Bioethics and Law*, Pieroma Press, Dublin, 2001; Susan Ryan-Sheridan, *Women and the New reproductive Technologies in Ireland*, Cork University Press, 1994; David Smith, *Life and Morality*, Gill & Macmillan, 1996; Kenneth Kearon, *Medical Ethics: An Introduction*, Columba Press, 1995.

47. Richard McCormick, *How Brave a New World?*, SCM Press, 1981. Chapter 9 'Rules for Abortion Debate', 176-188.

48. Patrick Hannon, 'Rules for the Debate', *The Furrow* 54 (February 2003): 67-74

49. Patrick Hannon, *Church, State, Morality and Law*, Gill and Macmillan, 1992

examined in the area of reproductive technologies. There is a need at this stage to move the discussion on by widening the parameters of the debate to include this question. In light of the proposals before the Government, society must engage the thorny issue of public policy. What should the content of legislation be in this disputed area of life? The moral positions have been clearly articulated and are unlikely to change. How can legislation respond to these strongly held moral positions on the status of the embryo and other issues? In a landmark statement in 1973, the Irish Catholic bishops recognised for the first time that the civil law need not coincide with the moral law as understood by the Catholic tradition: '[t]here are many things which the Catholic Church holds to be morally wrong and no one has ever suggested, least of all the Church herself, that they should be prohibited by the State.'[50]

This distinction needs to be again clearly articulated and promoted. The Catholic bishops have accepted that the legislator is obliged to protect and promote the common good of society rather than the moral stance of a particular community. Furthermore, they have accepted that individuals may differ in their understanding of what contributes to the common good and the flourishing of society. As a consequence, they encouraged individual citizens to come to their own conscientious decision about the content of the common good during the past referenda on divorce and abortion. *Dignitatis Humanae*, the Declaration on Religious Freedom, marked a decisive shift in the Catholic tradition's understanding of the relationship between church and state, law and morality. It recognised as fundamental the right to religious and moral freedom in society within limits set by public order in society. In promoting the principle of as 'much freedom as possible and as little constraint as is necessary'[51] it recognised that the exercise of human freedom contributes to the common good of society. The Declaration understood 'public order' to have a threefold content: justice, peace and public morality. Catholic contributors to the future debate will make a valuable contribution if they utilise the content and distinctions of the Declaration on Religious Freedom in their contributions to the public debate. Proposed legislation must be

---

50. See J. H. Whyte, *Church & State in Modern Ireland 1923-1979* [Second Edition], Gill & Macmillan, 1980. Chapter 13.
51. Declaration on Religious Freedom, 7.

evaluated by appeal to the demands of justice, peace and public morality. Though individuals will differ on the content of these realities, it does provide a framework and terminology that is enabling of rational discourse.

Finally, there is a need for a clear acceptance of religiously inspired argument in public debate. Persons whose worldview is shaped by the Christian vision of life can contribute to a rational debate on the formation of legislation. That vision provides them with an anthropology and an understanding of the world that shapes their rational discourse. Christian faith informs reason rather than replacing it.

CHAPTER THREE

The silent voice of creation and moral discourse

Amelia Fleming

As Christians, we are called to imbue all aspects of society with the Christian values of compassion for the weak and helpless. We purport to live in a moral society, co-existing with each other and the world around us, and yet humanity inflicts all kinds of cruelty on our fellow human beings as well as animals. Instead of images of God, we have become images of inhumanity. In the way the Triune God is a unity of equal communion in love, so too humanity should respect and welcome all of God's creation, for, as noted by St Thomas Aquinas, '[t]he whole universe together participates in the divine goodness more perfectly, and represents it better than any single creature whatever.'[1] Our responsibility within creation and our duty toward nature and the Creator is an essential part of our Christian faith.[2] I believe one of the major moral issues in contemporary Ireland is how we allow our animals and environment to be treated. Whatever we are responsible for is a matter of morality. If we are cruel to animals and abuse the environment it is a moral issue. We must begin to listen harder to creation's voice.

An ethical issue
The issues of animal cruelty and the ecological crisis may not seem like pressing ethical issues in the current Irish climate of sectarianism and escalating levels of violent aggression in criminal acts. However, as St Francis of Assisi noted, if there are those who will exclude any of God's creatures from the shelter of compassion and pity, there are those who will deal likewise with their brothers and sisters. In 1990, Pope John Paul II's message for the celebration of the World Day of Peace made reference to St Francis, and was entitled *The Ecological Crisis: A Common*

---

1. *Summa Theologica*, Prima Pars, question 48, ad 2.
2. Pope John Paul II, *The Ecological Crisis: A Common Responsibility*, 15.

Responsibility. In the message, Pope John Paul II noted that this patron saint of ecology offers Christians an example of genuine and deep respect for the integrity of creation. As a friend of the poor, who was loved by God's creatures, St Francis invited all creation to praise God. This poor man of Assisi gives us extraordinary witness that when we are at peace with God we are better able to devote ourselves to building up that peace with all creation, which is inseparable from peace among peoples. John Paul II observed that theology, philosophy and science all speak of a harmonious universe endowed with its own integrity, its own internal, dynamic balance. This teleological order must be respected. While we are called to explore this order, we must examine it with due care and make use of it, while safeguarding its integrity. He echoed the sentiments of St Francis when he stated in paragraph 13 that the seriousness of these issues clearly reveal the depth of humanity's moral crisis, explaining that if we lack an appreciation of the value of the human person and of human life, we will also lose interest in non-humans and in the earth itself. It is therefore important to engage in dialogue with each other about the world around us if we are to engage fully in Christian moral discourse. The necessity of this conversation has already been accepted and entered into in philosophical ethics, Irish secular society and, to a lesser extent perhaps, in the theological arena.

Cruelty to animals
In Ireland, there are an increasing number of reports of animal cruelty, in our national and local press. Many of these reports, following investigation, have reached our courts; cases of appalling neglect of not only domestic pets, but also cattle and sheep, where farmers have ignored Solomon's wise advise in Proverb 26:23 to know the condition of their flock well, and attend to their herd. Such farmers fail to inspect animals and farming equipment, permitting carcasses to remain unburied, and some are known to have injected slurry into cattle in order to interfere with diagnosis of bovine tuberculosis, to name but a few. Such incidents of cruelty are subject to the full force of the law, but this type of behaviour must be prevented from happening at all. It is no longer acceptable that we simply turn the page, and read on. Notwithstanding the fact that many people shower attention on their own pets, and yet show no compassion for animals consigned to the misery of ill-treatment and neglect, not

wanting to 'get involved', 'it's none of my business', part of the way society is, is because that is the way we want it to be. Turning a blind eye to cruelty is not optional. It is tantamount to complicit cruelty and to a sin of omission similar to that committed by Luke's priest and Levite on the road to Jericho (10:31-33). Deuteronomy teaches us that we must not ignore the plight of our neighbour's strayed or injured animals (22:1-5), and Exodus 23:4-5 instructs that this assistance should also be given to our enemy's oxen or donkeys, fallen under the weight of their load. It can be understandable why we would like to insulate ourselves from stories that upset or outrage us, but we should see this outrage as a form of knowledge. There is a reason why this is wrong. We know that this is wrong, and because we know that it is wrong, we ought to do something about it.

Supervision of children
It is of particular concern to all of us, if those responsible for cruelty towards animals are children. Worldwide studies have shown that children who are preoccupied with cruelty against animals are more likely to grow into violent adults. Such abuse of living creatures does not happen in a vacuum. Abusers themselves often suffer from low self-esteem, family abuse, and an inability to manage anger. Abuse is about power and control, regardless of the victim's species. A child can be provided with a sense of power and control in their cruelty towards animals. Although few such children do become a danger to society, this mode of behaviour should be a matter of concern for their parents. There should be a point made of re-educating the child about specific responsibility towards creatures. It should not be dismissed as 'mischief' or with a 'boys will be boys' attitude. (It is particularly teenage boys who are involved in abusive acts towards animals.) Collaboration between pet owners, animal shelter workers, veterinarians, educators and gardaí would promote awareness of the interconnection between violence against animals and people. This awareness is rooted in the Bible. In his temple discourse (7:1-8:3), Jeremiah recalls the sins listed in Exodus, and relates both the killing of innocent animals and human oppression of the weak: 'If you do not oppress the alien, the orphan, and the widow, or shed innocent blood in this place . . . then I will dwell with you in this place, in the land I gave of old to your ancestors forever and ever.' (7:6-7)

Responsibility for God's creation

We are all responsible for the whole of creation – humanity, the environment, wild animals as well as pets – the Bible calls it 'dominion' (Gen 1:28). However, it is not only Christians who are called to extol creation. We live in an increasingly pluralist society in which many people believe in God or gods, and believe in a form of perfect existence, whether it is heaven or nirvana. Due to Ireland's historical tradition of emigration, Irish society has not, until recently, experienced the reality of the multicultural social order and religious diversity resulting from migration inflows. However, a very different Irish society has emerged since the beginning of the asylum phenomena and the human trafficking of the 1990s. The Celtic Tiger was also highly influential, producing one of Europe's highest Gross Domestic Product growth rates and lowest unemployment ratios. In contemporary society, Christianity is no longer the sole religion in Ireland. All the major religions of the world are now represented, and notably, all teach compassion and love of animals: Islam teaches animal equality, Hindus denounce violence to animals, stemming from their belief that animal souls are the same as human souls. The first of the Buddhist faith's Five Precepts is not to harm sentient beings, as consciousness cannot be killed. All of these religions are useful when discussing the respect due to animals. However, I am approaching this particular issue of animal and environmental abuse from the Judeo-Christian perspective. Our Christian beliefs are based on ancient Jewish teachings as well as on Christ's life, death and resurrection.

When we look at the biblical basis for compassion towards animals, the Jewish notion of covenant is important. We are familiar with the covenants between God and humans, both of divine commitment and of human obligation, but there were also divine covenants with animals (Gen 9:9-10; Hosea 2:18). *Nefesh chaya* (the Hebrew term for a 'living soul') was applied to animals as well as humans, and Judaism included the concept of *tsa'ar ba'alei hayim* – the directive to prevent the 'sorrow of living creatures', for the 'righteous know the needs of their animals' (Prov 12:10). Humans came from dust like the other creatures of the flesh, though comparatively, God saw that humans were 'very' good and, before he rested after his work, he entrusted the whole of creation to the man and woman (Gen 2:3). We understand from this creation story, and New Testament texts, that

God made a covenant with humanity to manage and protect his creation, until his 'kingdom come', and that his will would be 'done on earth as it is in heaven' (Mt 6:10).

Stewards of creation

We are all stewards of the earth's resources and creatures (cf *The Catechism of the Catholic Church*, 2402) and as well as the original mandate to subdue the earth, there are other examples of stewardship in the scriptures, where someone handles the affairs of another. Abram had a steward, Eliezer of Damascus (Gen 15:2-3), and Joseph was Pharaoh's steward over the kingdom of Egypt in Genesis 41. In ancient kingdoms, a steward was a superior servant who ran the land in the king's absence, and upon his return, the steward was obliged to give full account of his actions. We too must be ready to give account of our actions regarding God's earthly kingdom. Our actions must stem from the kind of care and sense of responsibility that comes from shared ownership, and not merely management on behalf of another, with no real investment from us. This dominion is not absolute. It requires respect for the common good of all humanity, past, present and future. As the *Catechism* (2415) notes, 'Use of the mineral, vegetable and animal resources of the universe cannot be divorced from respect for moral imperatives.' We must recognise that there is interconnectedness in the created order. In the Christian worldview, there is disharmony between the human issues of justice, economics and creation because of sin – original, personal and social. We have broken our covenant with God. We are exploiting the earth. We exploit and abuse our fellow human beings, and we exploit and abuse our animals.

Perfect harmony

In contemporary society, the Christian makes faith-influenced moral decisions. We must balance our faith story with our scientific knowledge of evolution in order to make fully informed, conscientious decisions regarding our 'dominion' of creation. At the beginning of the Christian creation story in Genesis 1 and 2, there is a depiction of perfect harmony between humans, animals and the environment, with no violence. Vegetarianism was the first dietary law for all creation (Gen 1:29-30). It was only after sin and the Flood that meat was permissibly eaten by man, but with the restrictions of the kosher laws. However, we know that in the natural course of organic evolution, and as part of the natural food chain, some animals are carnivores, herbivores or omnivores, and require their natural diet in order to survive. The domestic cat, to take a very familiar example, cannot survive on a vegetarian diet alone, no matter what her owner's inclinations may be toward meat eating.

Ethical food production
God said, 'See, I have given you every plant yielding seed that is upon the face of all the earth, and every tree with seed in its fruit; you shall have them for food' (Gen 1:29).

For many reflective Christians in Ireland and around the world, the issue of animal cruelty becomes ethically unclear around questions of vegetarianism. It is apparent that though not all would agree that meat eating is immoral, there is an insistence that meat eating should be morally evaluated in the context of modern factory farming methods. We appear to have dissociated ourselves from the food on our plates, no longer seeing it as a slaughtered cow, lamb or pig, but simply as 'meat'. Because of our increasingly urban lifestyle in Irish society, many have become separated from agriculture, the land, and the terrible realities of meat production. In modern factory farming, all that is natural is denied the animal. Closely confined, they are force fed, many given hormones and antibiotics, and their babies (calves, chicks, lambs and piglets) are taken from them. The mothers of these young cry out in frustration just as a human mother would. An animal's needs and individuality disappear in this meat production, as it does in product testing, puppy farming (where dogs are used for the sole purpose of producing litters of puppies, non-stop, for human profit), and 'entertainment' such as circuses and hunting. I cannot see a morally correct relationship with the created world in this. There are many people who need to eat animals in order to survive, but countless meat eaters in the Western world have a choice between eating factory farmed meat and free range, compassionate meat production and choosing cosmetics that have not been tested on animals. The *Catechism* (2417) states that 'medical and scientific experimentation on animals is a morally acceptable practice if it remains within reasonable limits and contributes to caring or saving human lives', which echoes Jesus when he said that we are of more value than many sparrows (Lk 12:7), and much

more value than a sheep (Mt 12:11-12). However, cosmetic testing on animals, which is often cruel, does not save human lives,
and many Christians have moral qualms around medical labor-
atory experiments on monkeys and mice, for example, the
specifically bred 'onco-mouse' which develops cancer for research purposes, and the SCID (severe combined immuno defi-
ciency) mouse, which operates as a model of the human im-
mune system. For Christians who recognise the theological
meaning of 'sin', a change of mentality is required, a conversion.

Compassion towards all
In a sermon[3] written over 160 years ago, John Henry Newman
tried to convey those feelings which Christ's sufferings on the
cross for our sins should bring to us. Christ is the innocent Lamb
of God. For Newman, those feelings are the same emotions that
should stir in each person's heart on reading of cruelty towards
God's creatures in some chance publication that we take up, or
how it sometimes makes us shudder to hear of them. It is sad
that so little has changed since Newman's Victorian age that
when one reads this sermon, one realises that Newman could
have written it today. He speaks of the ill-treatment of livestock,
and of the cold-blooded, calculating acts of experimental science. Newman articulates, in his own inimitable way, how there
is 'something so very dreadful, so satanic in tormenting those
who have never harmed us, and who cannot defend themselves,
who are utterly in our power, who have weapons neither of
offence nor defence, that none but very hardened persons can
endure the thought of it'.

    As early as the fifth century, St John Chrysostom had argued
that surely we ought to show kindness and gentleness to animals for many reasons, chiefly because we are of the same
Creator. However, it was not until the 1990s that theologians
began to seriously engage with animals as a faith issue.
Interestingly, many of these were eco-feminist theologians who
had seen a connection between the status of women, racial inequality, the environment, and the spiritual significance of animals. Mainstream theology has to recognise the importance of
the respect and compassion due to God's creatures. God's compassion is over all that he has made (Ps 145:9). Happily, the

---

3. 'The Crucifixion', in *Parochial and Plain Sermons*, Vol VII, London,
Rivingtons, 1869, 136-7.

ranks of theologians examining our ethical responsibility towards animals and the environment continue to grow, with
Seán McDonagh SCC, being a notable Irish commentator.

There are those of us who love the individuality of animals
and include them in our personal lives, though they are without
rational souls. We house, feed and care for our pets. They are
our companions and confidantes, for whom we worry when
they are ill, and we often have to make agonising decisions
when confronted with an untreatable and painful condition. We
grieve and mourn their passing, experiencing a void in our lives.
We need to have such empathy and compassion for all living
creatures. Yet, there also needs to be a general theological recognition that a concern for animals is not just a matter of Christian
kindness, or of sentimentality. Due to the interconnectedness of
creation, it is also a matter of social justice. What we do to our
animals affects our environment and ourselves, and therefore
what we do is a matter of moral evaluation.

Exploitation of the so-called Third World
The injustice of the mass meat production industry crosses natural divides, affecting humanity, the environment, and animals.
Less well off countries such as India are satisfying western society's hunger for meat, of which Ireland is a part. In India, where
many people are hungry, one-third of arable land in that country is used to grow fodder for animals raised and slaughtered for
export. Animals raised for export in these poorer countries
means taking grain away from hungry people; furthermore, ani-
mal-intensive farming is an inefficient use of land and water because livestock waste about 90% of what they eat. Due to the EU
wide ban on feeding Meat and Bone Meal to livestock in the
wake of BSE (bovine spongiform encephalopathy) and nvCJD
(new variant Creutzfeldt-Jakob, the human disease thought due
to the same infectious agent as BSE), there is a high demand for
vegetable protein and non-genetically engineered feed like soy.
However, perhaps this protein food could be used for consumption by hungry human beings or be replaced by traditional plant
protein foods such as peas, beans and lentils. This would be
more beneficial to them than having more mouths to feed in the
form of livestock.

The injustice of the mass meat production industry and its
consequences also cuts across geographical divides. Brazil, like

India, exports soybeans to feed European cattle, pigs and poultry. The world's largest rain forest is being cleared to indulge our 'burger culture' in the west. The subsequent overgrazing and radical, unrestricted deforestation has ecological consequences, leading to climate change, land degradation, soil erosion by wind and water, flooding and possible future submersion of low-lying lands.

The word 'ecology' comes from the Greek *oikos*, meaning 'house', 'home' or 'place in which to live'. The earth and all it contains, and its place in the universe is the place in which we live, and we do so in a complex web of interrelated and interdependent dynamic systems. If we do not have an ethic of human responsibility and respect for these relationships, we will destroy our world and ourselves. As expressed in Hosea 4:3, the land will mourn and 'all who dwell in it languish, and also the beasts of the field and the birds of the air and even the fish of the sea' will be taken away. We must acquire a growing awareness of the fact that 'one cannot use with impunity the different categories of beings', whether these are living or inanimate, or make use of the natural elements simply as one wishes, according to one's own economic needs. It is quite the reverse. 'One must take into account the nature of each being and of its mutual connection in an ordered system, which is precisely the "cosmos".'

Our ecological responsibility
The ecological consequences of personal and corporate irresponsibility are global and local – everything must go somewhere, every action has a reaction. The pollutant effects of past individual CFC use of refrigerants and aerosol propellants were felt globally with the depletion of the ozone layer, and the related 'greenhouse effect' discovered in 1985. Acid rain falling and contaminating water and soil in Canada and Scandinavia originates from the industrial smoke stacks of the United States, England, Germany and Japan, as well as worldwide unrestricted deforestation and burning of fossil fuels. Locally, the Irish State has been found guilty by the European Court of Justice of seriously breaching an EU directive on waste management, including controls on illegal dumping. In 2004, the Irish Government was found to have failed 'over a protracted period of time' to establish an adequate and fully operational licensing system for waste disposal. Between 1997 and 2000, a dozen Irish citizens

had individually complained to the European Commission about the manner in which the State implemented and monitored waste disposal legislation.[4] These complaints were entered even before the once celebrated Garden County, Wicklow, had fallen victim to the illegal dumping of thousands of tonnes of toxic waste in 2002. Nearly one hundred illegal dump sites were identified, ranging from the quite small – a few black plastic bags in a ditch – to larger ones, at Coolnamadra and Whitestown near the Glen of Imaal, containing considerable amounts of commercial and industrial waste, and including hospital waste. Such was the extent of the environmental vandalism in these areas that the water table had been contaminated, polluting local groundwater and a nearby tributary of the River Slaney by leachate from the waste. If a growing number of individuals enter into dialogue and protest about these issues, the government and state bodies will be forced into debate and action.

In Ireland, the lyrical celebration of the beauty of our forty shades of green may soon become a traditional lament for times past, when the Irish countryside was full of small fields growing tillage crops like oats, turnips and wheat, or flax (once widely grown for linen production; when the same plant is grown for oil production it is called linseed) and rye. Today, the small amount of tillage farming undertaken consists mainly of huge fields of winter barley. Overgrazing, new farming practices including increased mechanisation, the cutting of silage instead of hay, and intensive farming, threaten plants such as meadow and marsh saxifrage, cottonweed, and rough poppy. Climatic changes, an increasing use of herbicides, and pressure from amenity use of land for recreation and tourism developments also aid this decline. The red grouse, hen harrier, grey partridge, and corncrake are among Ireland's declining wild bird species. The corn bunting is now officially extinct. Causes of their decline include habitat loss, reduction in food supplies, predation and poisonings from pesticides. The interrelatedness of creation is clear here. The Rural Protection Scheme (REPS) provides incentives to farmers to farm in an environmentally sustainable way, with enhanced levels of payment applying in Special Protection Areas (SPAs) and Special Areas for Conservation (SACs). Such incentives are valuable for this important lifestyle in order to protect and retain traditional farmland wildlife habitats and enhance the rural environment such as hedgerows and wetlands, which had been threatened by the intensified farming methods encouraged by the European Common Agricultural Policy. Subscribing to such an incentive also protects the farmer's income.

Soil instability is resulting in an alarming number of land-slides in the Irish countryside, such as the October 2003 Derrybrien landslide in County Galway. This incident caused severe damage to property and killed around 50,000 fish. In the same year, large amounts of peat and subsoil moved down the Dooncarton mountainside which overlooks several villages in north Mayo. Thousands of tonnes of mud and debris badly damaged Pullathomas graveyard. This destruction seemed to touch the public psyche in a way that fish kills and structural damage could not. An emotional wound had been opened with the wounds in the consecrated ground. Though the Dooncarton landslide followed heavy rain, soil stability can be weakened as a result of deforestation, intensive quarrying, illegal or irresponsible developments and intensive agricultural practices.

In his 1987 encyclical letter *Sollicitudo Rei Socialis*, paragraph 34, Pope John Paul II stressed the requirement to avoid types of development which result in pollution of the environment, with serious consequences for the health of the human population. We are morally obliged to protect natural, cultural, and coastal assets in danger. The land is a gift from God, given into our care at the beginning. *Gaudium et Spes* 57 declares that it is the human vocation as part of God's plan to 'till the earth to bring forth fruit and make it a dwelling place fit for all humanity'. Pope John Paul II also stressed in 1987 that land must 'be conserved with care since it is intended to be fruitful for generation upon generation' in order that each generation will inherit an even richer land.[5] We have a moral obligation to ourselves, our children and our children's children, to respect God's creation.

Accountability and education
I question our stewardship of Ireland and the world. Our country is listed by IUCN (International Union for the Conservation of Nature) and the Organisation for Economic Co-operation and Development (OECD in Environmental Indicators, 1996) as the worst achiever in the OECD, protecting the least amount of

5. 'The Pope's Homily in Rural America', *Origins*, Vol 9, No 18, xxx.

national territory for biodiversity.[6] The protection and conservation of our natural heritage depends on responsible action and the ethical behaviour of all stakeholders, business interests, communities and individuals as well Government and public authorities. It is regrettable that there is no published state policy on biodiversity in Ireland, though a National Biodiversity Plan was published in April 2002, which outlines a series of measures that will enhance biodiversity.

Biodiversity is the responsibility of the Heritage Policy Unit in the Department of Arts, Heritage and the Gaeltacht. Although this Unit is supported by the Heritage Council and is implemented by the Parks and Wildlife Service within Dúchas, it is the responsibility of all members of society to care for biodiversity and a healthy environment. Pope John Paul II calls for an urgent education in ecological responsibility: responsibility for oneself, for humans and non-humans, and for the earth.[7] It is the duty of the whole community to educate our younger members to be accountable for the ecological wellbeing of our world, be it through non-governmental and governmental organisations, or through an established Catholic education system, parish, or our own environmental behaviour. The first educator is the family, where the child learns to respect his/her neighbour and to love nature through parental example. It is within the family community of love that married couples are called to co-operate in God's creative activity by the procreation and education of children. This education should involve education in humanity, and the requirement to respect others and the world around us. Parents must lead by example by reducing household use of the earth's finite resources, and products which can damage the environment, reusing food waste by composting, and recycling aluminium, glass and paper, among many other environmentally friendly habits around the home.

Although education of the human person, for the human person is a life-long process of creative learning and growing in Christ, initiated by the lived morality of parents and others, it is continued formally in the classroom and lecture halls.

6. See address at the ESAI Biodiversity Conference, November 2000, by Shirley Clerkin, An Taisce entitled 'Current needs for policy to incorporate biodiversity considerations', available at http://www.antaisce.org/campaigns/policy_statements/biodiversity.pdf
7. Pope John Paul II, *The Ecological Crisis: A Common Responsibility*, 13.

Therefore, the Catholic educator has an important responsibility towards the formation and education of the young person's attitude toward creation, especially in a secular society where there is apathy towards religious and ethical formation. It is important that we teach the young adult to correctly and confidently use their Christian conscience in moral decision-making about their environment. It is significant that the Catholic educator is not only the religious educator in primary and secondary education systems, but is also the teacher of other Humanities subjects such as history, media and the CSPE (Civil, Social and Political Education) curriculum. The Catholic educator is also the lecturer of those other subjects such as philosophy, biology, biochemistry, genetics, geology and zoology in third level institutions. These areas raise questions about the human condition and the reality of life, moral issues which call for a judgement of conscience on the part of the student now or in later life. It is the role of the educator to fully inform the student conscience in order for it to make a reasoned ethical decision.

I cannot see how we are responsibly guarding our resources for the common good of future generations in our selfish consumerist culture. I cannot see how we can account for our actions when our King returns. In the words of the US Bishops, in their 1991 document *Renewing the Earth*, the web of life is one. Our own sacred dignity diminishes when we mistreat the natural world because we are going against what it means to be human as well as acting contrary to the common good. The Christian tradition demands of us the protection of humanity. It is increasingly clear that this cannot be separated from the care and defence of all of creation. The American astronaut James Irwin noted how, from space, the earth looks 'so fragile, so delicate, that if you touched it with a finger it would crumble and fall apart. Seeing this has to change a man, has to make a man appreciate the creation of God and the love of God ... My view of our planet was a glimpse of divinity.'[8]

---

8. cited by Cahal B. Cardinal Daly in *The Minding of Planet Earth*, (Dublin, Veritas, 2004), 169.

CHAPTER FOUR

A church silence in sexual moral discourse?

Raphael Gallagher CSsR

There is no end of conversation about sex in Ireland, and indeed about sexual morality. Silence begins to descend when Catholic sexual morality emerges as a topic: there may be some shouting and cross-talk, but hardly a conversation. The row dies down, and there is silence until the next spat. It is a curious sort of silence, somewhere between embarrassment and lack of interest. Trying to explain this silence demands some hypothesis. Mine is that there is a vacuum in Catholic Irish society, and thus in public forms of discourse, due to the way we have inherited and appropriated our religious legal system. Historically, the native Irish distrusted the English, including their public law. A lack of respect for public law did not necessarily mean that the natives were savages, quite the contrary. There were customs accepted at local level and a substratum of beliefs that had a profoundly civilising effect. The fact that the Renaissance had minimal effect in Ireland, however, exacerbated the vacuum when the English legal writ no longer held sway. Such Irish as could be classified as Renaissance people, like John Toland, usually lived abroad. When the state was founded the Catholic Church, unconsciously using a legal mindset that was more mediaeval than modern, filled the vacuum in public discourse. A country anxious to forge an identity and provide a forum for public exchange on moral issues readily accepted the legal presentation of Catholic doctrine. That mindset is no longer shared, hence the move towards silence on Catholic sexual morality as a public debating item.

Before the silence

The legal roots of Catholic sexual morality are not as narrow as sometimes portrayed. The Western legal tradition has its origin in the papal legal reform of the tenth and eleventh centuries. From the church point of view, law came to be seen as the essence of faith: God himself is law and therefore the law is dear to him. This view, taken from the *Sachsenspiegel*, the prototype book of German law published in 1220, helps to understand the sacred reverence given to church law.' Law was part of fulfilling the mission of the church on earth. While the subordinate position of secular law was implied, it was the church as a visible legal entity that was meant to control people for the next world by ensuring proper behaviour in the essential matters of this world. Church law became a means of reforming the world. This legal system provided the establishment of an external forum to balance the internal forum that already existed in the sacrament of penance.

The jurisdiction of the church was of such import that Thomas Becket was prepared to die for it instead of allowing King Henry II to interfere with what Becket considered essential to the freedom of the faith under the pope. No one would have argued that the canon law was perfect, since it was a human formulation, but it was as close as one could get to natural law and divine law. If the universe is subject to law, and this would have been agreed by all, then the supreme law should reflect as closely as possible God's design for the world. This explains why the church would have insisted on the supremacy of canon law over all other forms of law.

It is dangerous to summarise something so complex as the mediaeval papal revolution in so few words.[1] Easily forgotten could be the subtlety involved in the interpretation of canon law, and this was done by some of the most brilliant schoolmen of the age. Law was administered in the classic Roman mode, with a sense of equity: exceptions could be dealt with. The summary could also give the impression that other forms of law such as feudal law, mercantile law or royal law had no importance. They had, and often co-existed with canon law. But on one point there was no doubt allowed: canon law, because of its closer connection with natural and divine law, was supremely better because it guided the soul to heaven.

This may seem a long way from the silence about sexual morality of a Catholic type in Ireland. Let me return to my hypothesis. If Ireland, at the time of the foundation of the state,

---

1. A fuller account, on which my remarks are largely based, can be found in Harold J. Berman, *Law and Revolution. The Formation of the Western Legal Tradition*, Harvard University Press, Cambridge (Mass), 1983.

had no legal memory, so to speak, except to be 'against the foreigner's law', there was an obvious vacuum. Different types of
legal systems had developed in Europe after the collapse of
papal power (such as the rational, traditional or charismatic
forms, to use Weber's classification). If they had any influence in
Ireland, it was through the rule of the foreigner, and thus entirely
suspect. With the disappearance of the foreigner's rule, their
legal mindset was also set aside. The categories of discourse implied in the canon law of the church took over this vacuum and,
though this too was a foreign code of law, it was acceptable to a
people who had suffered 'for the sake of the Roman faith'.

Central to my hypothesis is the widespread acceptance of
these canonical categories for the interpretation of life. Just as
the political unification of the Catholic Church under a system
of law governed by papal authority could not have taken place
in the middle ages without a grassroots acceptance by the people, so too in Ireland after independence. I would not interpret
this as a supine attitude before a powerful hierarchy. The language made sense, not simply *faute de mieux*, but because it could
be seen as coherent, once one accepted the basic premises.
Canon law covered the essentials necessary for a good life, and it
did so working with theological categories that gave a judgement
on this life, and the next. Sexual morality was not simply
couched in legal terms: these legal terms had a theological background that gave them legitimacy in the eyes of God.

Without the fear of hell, the worry about purgatory and the
hope of heaven, it is impossible to understand the origins of the
Western legal tradition in general or the reason why a revived
form of it, in canon law, had such a powerful effect in Ireland.
The promulgation of the Code of Canon Law in 1917 and the
achievement of a partial independence some five years later
may not be coincidental in explaining how a particular Catholic
legal system filled a vacuum in terms of sexual morality.

If all of life, including its sexual aspect, can be both controlled
and interpreted through canon law, then the rejection of its powers has a far-reaching effect. That is the hypothesis I propose
about the inability of the church to speak publicly now, with
conviction, on sexual matters in Ireland. Other categories have
taken over, the language of human rights being the most obvious one. The world of sexuality interpreted though a medieval
conception of law, and underpinned by a particular theology of

heaven, hell and purgatory, no longer convinces. There are other ways of explaining sexuality, and the problem for the church is in coming to understand these new languages. Meanwhile there is a silence because the new language is foreign to the heritage of an Irish church formed by canon law with its roots in a medieval conception of heaven, hell and purgatory.

A contemporary complication
There is a complicating factor, however. I presume that public conversations on Catholic sexual morality would at least acknowledge that such a morality has a religious component. The collapse of the canonical ways of dealing with sexuality coincides, in Ireland, with the growth of the view that religious based discourse is no longer proper in the public square. The emergence of this view has its own historical roots. The modern states, which took form in the seventeenth and eighteenth centuries after the bitter wars of religion, were in varying degrees philosophically conceived and practically arranged so that religion would not be considered part of political life. The secularisation of politics has had long-term effects. They are not to be seen in the immediate aftermath of the foundation of the Irish state, but it seems that they shape the current prevailing view. Politics is politics, and religion is religion: the two should not be mixed. While there was a mode of public conversation on sexual matters during the period where canon law held sway, the collapse of this mode has occurred precisely at an historical period where religious-based views are considered to be private matters, and thus not proper for a public conversation. This argument rests on the assumption that while religion may be deeply significant to people's personal lives it does not necessarily have public consequences.[2] The world can be understood in terms of economic policies, political arrangements, military strategies and social procedures to regulate democracies. These are the stuff of public discourse, but not religion. This does not seem to me to be very wise, but such is the current general perception. It is not very wise: the world flashpoints of the last decade, from terrorism to fundamentalism, are proving intractable precisely

---

2. This argument is more fully examined in Heather Windows, 'Religion as a Moral Source: Can religion function as a shared source of moral authority in a liberal democracy?', *Heythrop Theological Journal* XLV (2004), 197-208.

because politics has lost the art of public discourse about religious-based values. Though not wise, it is the prevailing view of public life. Thus, even when the church in Ireland wishes to speak publicly about Catholic sexual morality, it is doing so within a society that is not convinced that religious-based views are public debating points.

Are we condemned to be silent?
The omens are clearly not good for a public conversation about Catholic sexual morality given my hypothesis that the collapse of a canonically based view has coincided with an epoch when religious-based views are not particularly welcome in the public political forum. The impasse on Catholic sexual morality will be broken only by a closer analysis of the basis of how Catholic moral norms are given a foundation. This will have the advantage of moving the debating point from the public forum, at least initially, to its more proper home: a consideration of what is good for the human person in the first place.

Following Charles Taylor,[3] this difficulty in giving a foundation for morality can be interpreted as a divergence about moral sources, or the constitutive goods, which form the modern moral person. I take the sources of morality to mean, in this context, those values which are at the basis of our moral ideals and practical actions. Traditionally, these sources were seen as exterior to the individual person: that is true of the philosophic systems of Plato and Aristotle as it is clearly also true of the revealed sources of morality developed by Christianity.

What is novel, and broadly coincident with the problems I have indicated in Ireland, is that the sources for morality are now considered to be internal to the human person. Typically, the contemporary person does not seek the sources for a good moral life outside themselves, but within. This happens in two different ways. One way of seeking an internal source for the moral life, which obviously includes our sexual options, is to see our human intelligence as a practical instrument that helps us to calculate what choices to make in life. A second line of internal searching, no less important than the first, is to look into our interior lives and decide on the basis of what is likely to be the most fulfilling choice in terms of being true to myself. Both these

---

3. Especially his classic book *Sources of the Self*, Harvard University Press, Cambridge (Mass), 1989.

forms of placing the sources of morality within ourselves, as distinct from reliance on outside sources, deserve a comment in
terms of the current difficulties for the church on sexual morality
in public debate.

Take the first view, where human intelligence is seen as a
personal instrument to shape one's life. The problem is not with
having a high view of the gift of intelligence: the debating point,
for this essay, is whether this intelligence is simply subject to its
own internal laws. I think there is substantial evidence, in the
sexual area, to show that this is what is generally accepted. If
something can be done, without harming others intentionally,
then go and do it. I am not so much thinking of a hedonistic view
of life, however problematic that may be too, so much as the impact of technology on sexual patterns of behaviour. It is now
possible to control fertility, and to avoid sexually transmitted
diseases, if one thinks about it. In advance. Behaviour is not dictated by norms imposed from outside, but by a prior perception
of what is good for myself. If I use my intelligence, I can control
my body, and my body is my own to control. Clearly the cosmological worldview of a canon law based on theological presump-
tions about heaven, hell and purgatory does not enter this type
of equation.

In the second view, the search for an internal sourcing of sexual morality is even more obvious. The important thing in life is
to be true to my own feelings and to be authentic in the sense
that the choices I make in life are mine, and no one else's. Once
again, I do not think we should take issue with the importance
of being aware of and accepting our own choices in life. That
seems fundamental. What is novel, however, is the view that the
moral criteria (or the sources of morality) are entirely to be
found in the realm of my personal sentiments and feelings.

What is interesting, in considering a public language for
Catholic sexual morality, is that these new forms interiorising
the sources of moral judgement may be in conflict with themselves as well as obviously not consonant with traditional views.
The utilitarian view (my body is my own and I am intelligent
enough to know what to with it) does not sit easily with the
post-romantic view (my body is the source of my feelings and I
must listen attentively to what it is telling me). But the point
they have in common, a greater respect for the individual person as a moral subject, may be more fruitful territory for public

conversations that at first appears. The breakdown of the externally imposed common language of the canonical books may be providential after all.

The inability to hold public conversations about Catholic sexual morality thus emerges as a problem of competing languages. The attempts at debate degenerate into shouting games because there is not a shared language. I have identified three variants. There is a residual language from the canon law tradition, and this usually identifies sexual morality as a question of norms and codes. Two new competing voices have emerged, one stressing the technological view of sex and the other more reliant on an emotional interpretation of what is considered good behaviour. Because the new voices are subjective, in the sense that the sources on which their arguments are based are interior to the individual, they are impatient with the normative language of the Catholic Church that is seen as an outside intrusion on personal freedom. Even the upholders of normative religious views on sexual matters would grant that there is more to be discussed than legal codes, but they have lost the language to communicate in an Ireland no longer religiously shaped by canon law. Their silence is thus the silence of strangers in a foreign land, speaking a language the natives do not know.

What is there to talk about?
I grant that people representing the new sources for morality are probably quite happy that the church is no longer interfering, or at least that its interventions are kept to the margins. How can I justify the recovery of a public voice?

This can be justified only on the basis of excluding certain positions. There can be no return to the view that Catholic moral norms should dictate the law of the land. Catholicism cannot function, either in theory or in practice, as a shared moral source for sexual morality in a culturally diverse Ireland. That point is clearly established theologically, and it has political consequences.[4] It has to be some form of shared moral reasoning, and not the fact that some actions are forbidden by the church, which provides the authority to establish public sexual norms. But this could beg the question: can we not have this form of shared moral reasoning without recourse to the Catholic tradition of

---

4. Patrick Hannon, *Church, State, Morality and Law*, Gill and Macmillan, Dublin, 1992.

arguing in moral matters? Though I have acknowledged that the current view in Ireland seems to favour an exclusion of religious based views from public debate, I have also entered a caveat that I do not think it is a very wise position. This deserves a further comment.

It is interesting that John Rawls, certainly an articulate exponent of a theory of liberal democracy organised on rational criteria, now seems more open to the possibility of religious considerations being a proper part of public debate in liberal democratic states.[5] He does so with a proviso. If a religious inspired view is being proposed as a suitable basis for social organisation, it must be accompanied by what he calls appropriate public reasons. Religious arguments are not *per se* excluded, according to Rawls in his later views, but only those religious reasons may be put forward which are capable of being communicated through the rules of public rational debate. This is an important clarification. The Catholic Church could claim a voice in public debate on sexual morality in Ireland if we followed through on this suggestion. The basis of any argument proposed would not be that such and such is the teaching of the church, but that sexual mores have public consequences which can be identified independently of the views of church authority. There would have to be agreement on what these consequences might be: one could propose the general common good of society, a respectful tolerance for the views of others and adequate care for the support of family-based institutions. This is clearly a limited list, and obviously is not meant as an agenda. I use it as an example. There are aspects of sexual morality, such as these three, which are a core concern of the general social fabric. The Catholic Church has views on these, and when such views are presented in terms of the issues themselves (thus, not on the basis of church teaching or authority claims) the public debate could be enhanced. To do this, however, will demand a substantial shift in the presentation of Catholic sexual morality. What has collapsed in Ireland, in the sense of not being welcomed in the public forum, is the normative residue of the canon law tradition on sexual moral-

5. Compare the views of John Rawls in *The Law of Peoples*, Harvard University Press, Cambridge (Mass), 1999 with his earlier views as expressed in *A Theory of Justice*, Harvard University Press, Cambridge (Mass), 1971.

ity.[6] Irish society has its own reasons for this rejection. It is my view that the rejection is not the great disaster it seems to many because sexual discourse cannot be reduced to conversations about norms and laws. The fabric of sexual identity and the tortuous path of sexual development are far too complex to be boxed into normative conversations. The recovery of a voice for the Catholic Church, more or less following the criteria of Rawls, will thus depend on the ability of the church to present its sexual moral views in a more inclusive way than has been the case.

To whom are we talking?
Getting to this position will not be easy. The collapse of a canonically based form of sexual norms left a void primarily within the church, and only then in Irish society given the prominent place of the church. I have the impression that the church, aware of the unresolved tensions about sexual morality within its own community, then tried to rely to political strategies to ensure the imposition of views consonant with its traditional teaching. The reversal of this trend means that the first partners for public dialogue should be within the church. If this conversation yields significant results it will be possible to see what aspects of sexual morality are germane to public political debate, and which are not. It will also ensure a measure of coherence between church morality and its contribution to the public debate: too often there is an impression of double-speak in this regard.

The question to be addressed, on an internal church level, is the correlation between norms and experience. The significance of sexuality is in proportion to its perceived significance. Of course, sexuality involves bodily desires that we can analyse on their own terms: equally, sexuality can be formulated in a normative way that can also be the subject of further considerations. The deeper meaning of sexuality, however, is shaped by the grammar, syntax and linguistic context in which bodily desires and normative formulae find their home. This is the heart of the matter. We have momentarily lost the ability to use an inclusive grammar of sexuality; its meaning is reduced either to the swirling plane of physical desires or the colder corner of norm-

---

6. The process is documented in Tom Inglis, *Moral Monopoly. The Catholic Church in Modern Irish Society*, Gill and Macmillan, Dublin, 1987 (1st edition).

ative formulations. It is no solution to urge, as Lady Bennerley[7] did, that the only way to be happy is to forget our body and then time passes quickly without further anxiety. The normative or legal way of dealing with the question is just as unpromising. The paradox here is that the liberalisation of sexual norms and laws, as has been the case in Ireland, still reduces the complex world of sexuality to a level of flatness where chastity may be seen as no more a virtue than malnutrition. The vacuum thus reveals itself for what it is: the lack of a symbolic language for sexuality. Rollo May's observation is pertinent: people can have so much sex but so little meaning in their lives. We need to recover the lost voices of the Catholic tradition if we are to escape from the reduction of sexual talk to a normative level. This was always problematic, but even more so when the consensus on the norms has gone.[8]

The grammar of our public language
I started with the hypothesis that one cause of the church's inability to engage in fruitful public debate on sexual morality is associated with the way a particular legal tradition of Catholicism took root in the nascent Irish state. The thesis I propose is that the alienation that this provoked in the long term could be addressed by a grammar of sexuality that is inclusive in its scope and integrative in its application. This involves a journey of retrieval: behind the canonical norms what was there, besides the particular notions of heaven, hell and purgatory that I alluded to?

The original vision is one where the allied aspects of sexuality, human loneliness and the natural desire for children, are integrated. In the twin accounts of the Book of Genesis the earlier Yahwist tradition (circa 950 BC) alludes to the linkage between our sexual nature and our inner emptiness: it is not good that the human person be alone (Gen 2:24). The later Priestly tradition (circa 550 BC), possibly reflecting a warrior agricultural nation's need for a workforce and soldiers, stressed the social role of our

---

7. A minor character in D. H. Lawrence, *Lady Chatterley's Lover*, London, 1928.
8. The question is wider than sexual morality: the root question is a religious one. Confer Patrick Riordan, 'Permission to speak: Religious arguments in public reason', *Heythrop Theological Journal* XLV (2004), 178-196.

sexual nature: be fruitful and multiply (Gen 1:18). The retrieval has to be a full retrieval; otherwise the public discourse of the church on sexuality will continue its alienating path. The perception that the church has reduced the tradition to norms about procreation alone is well known: another strand in the tradition, more obvious in recent times, is the reduction of sexual desire to what is pleasurable and thus a way of lessening our loneliness. The starting point of the public grammar of sexual discourse is a retrieval of the fuller originating vision.

Complementing this retrieval, the grammar will then demand a mode of confronting the residue of the two forms of reductionism just mentioned. Reducing sex to procreation only, or simply to pleasure, is personally alienating: it leads logically to an alienated society given that we cannot understand the human person except as one who is constitutively social. The aspect of the social alienation that is most obvious is the influence of technology on sexual mores. I am not merely thinking of contraception or the now easy access to pornography. The influence is deeper and more corrosive. The technological mode of thinking, linked to the utilitarian sourcing of morality that I referred to, typically sees sex as a thing to be done, another performance that will ensure our identity. 'Having sex' strikes me as a most curious combination of ideas, as if it were the equivalent of having a job or a meal. It is interesting that Masters and Johnson, not known defenders of the Catholic moral tradition, share the same reservation: 'Sex, like work, becomes a matter of performance. There is always a goal in view, ejaculation for the man, and orgasm for the woman. If these goals are achieved, the job has been satisfactorily performed … sex for them is not a way of being, a way of expressing identity or feeling or a way of nourishing a commitment. It is always a single incident, an occasion, an accomplishment … goal-oriented sex is self-defeating. Sex interest is soon lost as a result of the performance demand.'[9]

The grammar of sex must be capable of addressing these issues. A reduction of that grammar to canonical norms has clearly failed in Ireland. What has filled the ensuing vacuum needs to be examined. It is not my agenda to suggest a reduction of sexual language to religious language: those days of the primitive religions, where the two great mysteries of life were intertwined to

9. William Masters and Virginia Johnston, *Sex isn't that simple*, Strauss and Giroux, New York, 1974, 90.

the extent that the sex life of the gods was a key myth, are of interest but hardly of moral relevance now. My concern is to suggest that the religious language and sexual language could be re-united. The competing voices in Irish society may seem unpropitious territory for this to happen. Perhaps we are being too hasty in dismissing the new voices? The sexual and sacral worlds can be close, not in the sense of primitive religions, but in the light of our search for interpersonal comprehension. The public linkage between sexual and religious questions is easily demonstrable in the excesses of sexist language: if God is portrayed in a straitjacket patriarchal uniform, it is logical that our presentation of revelation and church teaching will be similarly flawed.

And what are they talking about?
The recovery of a public voice for the church in sexual debates thus indicates a surprising possibility. The talk will be less about sex than about religion as a persistent phenomenon in society. How the church deals with sexual morality among its own members will be a matter for the church community in the light of its own doctrine. The surprise is how the foundations for this doctrine, the sacred scriptures, have little to say about sexual morality but much to say about how society could benefit morally from a covenanted view of life where particular social values (such as love, mercy, forgiveness, solidarity with the stranger) could shape the way we relate to each other, including sexually.

An example may be useful before I offer my conclusion. Living together before marriage is largely accepted in Ireland, a clear rejection of the previous canonical prohibition to do so. There is some debate about this in theological journals,[10] but little public conversation in the church community. Yet, surely, it is an issue that affects not just church doctrine but how Irish society is being shaped. We could be going through a cultural period when the definition of marriage, both theologically and socially, needs to be reformulated. This, surely, is an example where the public voice of the church should be heard, not to impose a part-

---

10. An example is the exchange of views between Lisa S. Cahill and Michael G. Lawler on the theological interpretation of cohabitation in *Theological Studies* 64 (2003), 78-105 (Cahill's views) and *Theological Studies* 65 (2004), 623-629 (Lawler's views).

icular moral view, but to contribute towards the construction of a new social consensus on key issues that affect family structures. Facing such issues I am in agreement with Octavio Paz: 'Every time a society finds itself in crisis it instinctively turns its eyes towards its origins and looks there for a sign.'[11] The remote origins of the canonical approach to sexual morality, whose collapse provoked the silence of the church, could be a useful debating point with the voices that have dominated since that collapse. The silence of the church on sexual questions is worrying, not because it is a sexual silence, but because it is symptomatic of the church's inability to explain the significance of a religious approach to life.

11. Octavio Paz, 'Reflections: Mexico and the United States', *The New Yorker*, 17 September 1979, 153.

CHAPTER FIVE

Moral discourse and journalism

Donal Harrington

'Discourse' means serious conversation – that much is straight-forward. The words 'morality' and 'journalism', however, are multivalent. That in turn complicates the relationship between the two. This essay has the modest aim of clarifying some of that complexity so as to yield a perspective on the relationship between morality and journalism today. This essay has four parts. In the first three I consider the terms 'culture', 'morality' and 'journalism' in turn. I will be working towards suggesting some correspondence in the evolving meaning of each of the terms. Fourthly, I will reflect on what light the preceding discussion throws on the kind of discourse we might be talking about.

My own interest in this area was originally sparked by Patrick Hannon. I recall a meeting of moral theologians some-time in the late 1980s where he gave a presentation on a short course he taught on ethics and communications. I was inspired to go off and develop a course on this subject myself. I was also struck – and continue to be – by how little interest moral theology shows in the ethics of communications relative to other areas of moral discourse.

I. CULTURE

A distinction is made between pre-modern (classical), modern and post-modern culture. To some extent it is a chronological sequence. But in many ways the three co-exist and interact in how we experience and interpret our world and how it interprets us.

Pre-modern Culture

In the pre-modern or classical sensibility, God is at the centre. The ancient meaning of 'justice' – the Greeks' *diké* and the Jews' *sedaqah* – reflects this. There is a divinely originated order to the world, to which we humans are subordinate. Antigone's famous lines to Creon reflect it: 'Nor did I think your orders were so strong / That you, a mortal man, could overrun / The gods' un-written and unfailing laws.' Pre-modern culture is also 'classi-cal' in the sense of Lonergan's distinction between a classicist worldview and historical-mindedness. In its classical sense cult-ure was unchanging and uniform. There was one true culture to which one aspired, to become a person of culture or a cultured person.

Modern Culture

Modern culture emerged out of the breakdown of classical cult-ure. It was prepared for in the Renaissance discovery of 'human-ism', in the Reformation's spelling the end of 'Christendom', in the gradual rise of what we know as modern science. It is cap-tured in the idea of 'Enlightenment', with its vivid sense of humanity coming to a new realisation about itself and about its potential.

I recall a novel wherein there was an imaginative retelling of the creation story (I think it was Bruno Schultz, *Sanatorium under the Sign of the Hourglass*). God was happily creating away until the final day when God felt the strange texture of what had just newly been created that day. Uneasily, God's hand withdrew. 'Enlightenment' has a sense of humanity itself coming to the same strange discovery of the power of its own freedom.

As we speak about modern culture we think particularly of the power of human rationality in the technological sense. The machine is one dominant symbol of modern culture and of hum-anity's imposing its own stamp on what was originally God's creation. Where previously we sought to understand God's ways, now we have matured to the point of imposing our own patterns.

Post-modern Culture

While some speak of post-modernity as a third stage, others speak of it as a further development within modernity, whether it be 'late modernity' or a crisis within modernity or the 'within-ness' of modernity. This suggests aspects both of continuity and of discontinuity. Post-modern sensibility includes within it a disenchantment with modernity's prizing of technological rationality and trusting in emancipation through its power. It in-cludes a rejection of meta-narratives in their attempt to explain everything (including the meta-narratives of modernity itself).

Related to this, it includes a prizing of difference and diversity – the category of 'the other'. Also related, it brings the ephemeral and the immediate to the centre of human consciousness and living.

Perhaps one could put the transition from classical to modern to post-modern like this. Once there was 'the Truth'. Then there was a sense of there being a 'Truth' but also that, in Janet Soskice's phrase, 'the truth looks different from here'. Then there was the sense of 'my truth' and 'your truth', but no 'Truth'. Richard Kearney, in his study of imagination, offers the following progression. In classical culture, imagination was like a mirror held up to the divine order. In modern culture, imagination is likened to a lamp, finding its own way forward. In postmodern culture, it is like a labyrinth of mirrors, an endless regression of reflections of reflections of reflections, with no source. It is as if, in Plato's cave, there is no Sun, only the shadows.

II. MORALITY

I want now to suggest shifts in our understanding of morality that have at least some correspondence to the emergence of modernity and post-modernity out of the prior classical culture.

Objective morality
A classical sense of morality is already to the fore in the description of the pre-modern above. Morality was 'objective' in the sense of being prior to human reason, something of divine origin and which was discovered rather than invented by humanity. This is reflected in some traditional understandings of 'the ten commandments' and 'the natural law' as articulating a divinely-decreed way of behaving.

Woody Allen's film *Crimes and Misdemeanours* captures it. In the film, a man wishes to end his affair but the woman threatens to tell his wife. The man arranges with his brother, a criminal type, to have her taken care of. The film rides on this theme: does it matter, after all, whether you deal with things in such a way? Or is there indeed a moral order to the universe?

Morality as pragmatism
Modern culture is inseparably bound up with the development of capitalism. Adam Smith's *The Wealth of Nations* came in 1776. Also, it seems to me, a significant part of the mix is the 'social

contract' thinking from those times. Capitalism developed at a time when philosophy was talking about human beings being social, not by nature, but by contract. When the two merge, it issues in the idea that human beings have no moral obligations to one another other than those imposed by the law – a law which they themselves have created and assented to in the interests of their own individual prospering. There is nothing beyond the law to curb the pursuit of self-interest.

Johann Baptist Metz has spoken of how, with the Reformation, religion ceases to be the basis of the political unity of the state. The new principle which is to regulate and underpin social relationships is the principle of exchange. All other values recede into the private individual realm. Production, trade and consumption are everything. Buying-and-selling has become the paradigmatic human relationship. There is still a meta-narrative, but its God is now the God of endless progress.

In this context morality becomes pragmatism. As Alisdair Macintyre would put it, the principle of excellence has given way to that of efficiency. As Stephen Covey presents it, there has been a shift from human character to human technique. When technical efficiency supplants excellence of character, pragmatism has supplanted morality.

Does utilitarianism fit in here, an attempt to recast morality in the absence of any objective moral order? Actions have utility value and the best actions are those that produce the best results. But without a reference point for 'best', the whole enterprise falls under the power of pragmatic considerations of what the best results are.

Morality as Aesthetics

In the context of post-modernity morality can manifest itself as something akin to aesthetics. Against a backdrop of no meta-narrative, there is no talk of life's ultimate value. Morality, then, is very much a case of 'my truth' and 'your truth'. It is about crafting a life, inventing a self – aesthetics in that sense. It is about what feels right for me.

There is something in this of post-modernity's focus on the ephemeral, as witnessed, say, in its pre-occupation with shopping and fashion and play. Nor is capitalism absent here, its art now lying in the manipulation of taste and fashion and desire. Zygmunt Baumann offers the images of the vagabond and the tourist:

The vagabond is a pilgrim without a destination; a nomad without an itinerary. The vagabond journeys through an unstructured space; like a wanderer in the desert, who knows only of such trails as are marked with his own footprints, and blown off again by the wind the moment he passes, the vagabond structures the site he happens to occupy at the moment, only to dismantle the structure again as he leaves. Each successive spacing is local and temporary – episodic.

It is the tourist's aesthetic capacity – his or her curiosity, need of amusement, will and ability to live through novel, pleasurable and pleasurably novel experiences – which appears to possess a nearly total freedom of spacing, the tourist's life-world … The tourists pay for their freedom; the right to disregard native concerns and feeling, the right to spin their own web of meanings, they obtain in a commercial transaction.[1]

But there is another thread. Post-modernity's interest in difference and diversity – in 'the other' – yields a contrasting moral experience. The other is the different but it is also 'the face', the other that calls on me. Somewhere between the classicist's moral universals and the relativistic 'my truth', there is the sense of strong, perhaps indissoluble connections between the quality of response to the other and the quality of one's own becoming.

This thread ties in with some contemporary Christian ethical writing. Daniel Maguire and Edward Schillebeeckx, for instance, both see the foundational moral experience to lie in this 'call' of the other as other. In both there is a sense of this as spiritual and not just moral. Again, Hans Küng writes of a convergence of the great world religions in a 'global ethic' whose fundamental demand is that each human being be treated humanely.

III. JOURNALISM

I would like to use the above, summary as it is, as a context, a set of concepts, that might yield a perspective on journalism today. But first, a word on journalism itself. Journalism today seems to me to be, not so much a univocal term, as something of an umbrella term that covers different, contrasting and even contradictory realities. There are the likes of John Pilger, in whom the journalist resembles almost an Old Testament prophet. And there is

---

1. *Postmodern Ethics*, Oxford, Blackwell, 1993, 240-241.

the latest excess of the tabloid press. The two go by the name of journalism and there is all kinds of everything in between.

Here, morality and journalism are in the same boat. It is clear from the previous section that 'morality' too has different, even markedly different meanings. In each case it is as if one almost has to begin the conversation by asking, *à la* Macintyre, 'whose morality, which journalism?'

So, developing from the previous sections, I am going to outline three perspectives on journalism. I don't intend this as a neat fit (or a chronological fit) with the three experiences of culture or the three experiences of morality already outlined. There may, nevertheless, be some correspondence.

Journalism as Public Service
Classically, journalism has been conceived as a public service. It is a valued part of a democratic society. It contributes to an informed and politically literate and critical public. It exists for the public benefit. Its loyalty is to the community. Its concern is for the truth. It feels the weight of social responsibility. There may be more of a feel of this in the provincial press and local radio than in much of the national media. But it is also reflected where broadcasting stations are financed by government licence fees. It is the sense that journalism is 'ours', an aspect of what we are and an instrument of our becoming.

Journalism as Market Reality
There has been a huge shift in modern times from journalism as a public service to journalism as a market reality. While the two roles co-exist, more and more the former is giving way to the latter. Increasingly, journalism is about selling rather than serving. The bottom-line is profit. This is perhaps the dimension that is absent from journalism's ethical reflections on itself, such as the NUJ's ethical code. For instance, that code states a standard regarding the invasion of privacy. But if one newspaper intrudes on privacy in a given instance and another does not, the code has no explanation of why one does and the other does not. It lacks analytic power.

The explanation comes only when one highlights the context in which journalism operates. And that context today is a market context. The operating of journalism is not clarified simply by referring to the ethical parameters. Rather journalism's observance or otherwise of its own ethical standards is more and more determined by pragmatic market considerations. Ethics is subsumed by the pragmatics of profit and of survival.

Imagine a situation where a commercial organisation obtains feedback that one of its products is regarded out there as environmentally unfriendly. The decision is made to remove the product because it has been revealed to be unethical to continue with it. But the real reason has nothing to do with ethics. It is good business to remove products that consumers react against. If the consumers decided to like the same product again, would there still be talk of ethics?

The point of the example translates to the world of journalism. As a market reality journalism operates on the pragmatic principle of telling the audience what they want to hear. Buying-and-selling is the overarching context. Buying and selling happen when people are being told what they want to hear.

The market thus undermines whatever internal goals around public service previously characterised journalism. The driving force is about satisfying the preferences of the consumer. Values around truth and information are relegated. The first commandment is to deliver eyeballs to advertisers.

Journalism as Entertainment

Earlier I remarked on how post-modernity is sometimes described as the 'withinness' of modernity. In similar fashion, journalism as market reality has entertainment as its inner core. This in turn corresponds closely to post-modernity's focus on the ephemeral and superficial.

I recall one radio journalist remarking on his frustration here. He was keen at the time to generate some serious discussion of unemployment on the programme. But he could do very little; the topic, in the vocabulary of the profession, was not 'sexy'. In other words, it lacked entertainment value.

Even the news itself – which we would presume to be the profession at its most serious – has to be entertaining. Competition demands it. The relationship is tenuous between what is important in the world and what is the headline in the news. In their study, Klaidman and Beauchamp illustrate the point as follows:

> The need for action and pictures to hold the attention of a viewing audience also plays an important part in determining what television covers and how it covers the events se-

lected for inclusion ... Here a judgement about what most viewers want to watch, and how much of it they want, more often determines what news will be broadcast – or at least the length at which it will be broadcast – than judgements about the intrinsic importance of the events or data.[2]

Here I draw on the analysis of George Steiner for the way in which it captures the spirit of post-modern journalism. He speaks of journalism as the genius of the age, as 'an epistemology and ethics of spurious temporality'.

Journalistic presentation generates a temporality of equivalent instanteity. All things are more or less of equal import; all are only daily. Correspondingly, the content, the possible significance of the material which journalism communicates, is 'remaindered' the day after. The journalistic vision sharpens to the point of maximum impact every event, every individual and social configuration; but the honing is uniform. Political enormity and the circus, the leap of science and those of the athlete, apocalypse and indigestion, are given the same edge. Paradoxically, this monotone of graphic urgency anaesthetizes. The utmost beauty or terror are shredded at close of day. We are made whole again, and expectant, in time for the morning edition.[3]

This indeed reflects the post-modern focus on trivia and sensation. Increasingly we exist in order to be entertained. We are constantly moved on from one sensation to another more novel – Baumann's 'novel, pleasurable and pleasurably novel experiences'. But it is all part of the logic of capitalism and its manipulation of taste. So much is this the dynamic that it has been suggested that post-modernity may essentially be little else than the latest stage in capitalism.

But there is more. Just as we saw two strands to the postmodern experience of morality, so there is another strand to journalism in the post-modern context. Martin Bell recounts a story from the Bosnian conflict that captures it. One particular journalist wanted to do a piece about a sniper. He gained access and ended up hiding with the sniper behind a rock. He asked the sniper what did he see. The sniper said he saw two people walking down the road and asked the journalist, 'Which of them

2. *The Virtuous Journalist*, Oxford, Oxford University Press, 1987, 73-74.
3. *Real Presences*, Chicago, University of Chicago Press, 1991, 26-27.

do you want me to shoot?' Too late the journalist realised what
he had got into. As he made his excuses and began to depart he
heard two shots ring out. He looked around to hear the sniper
say, 'Pity, you could have saved one of them'.

Bell uses the story to speak about what he calls 'the journalism of attachment'. There is more to journalism than the market-
driven urge to entertain. There is also the person of the journalist. There is his or her sense of the 'other', the 'face' – a sense that
is sometimes submerged and which sometimes, as in the story,
asserts itself.

When it does, journalism is operating against the backdrop
of some kind of intuition of the *humanum*, of what is right when
it comes to human beings because they are human beings. The
sense of the other is our intuition as to who we are. In that, it is
also our sense of 'truth'. Here there is the possibility of a meta-
narrative, different from the exclusivist and externally-imposed
meta-narratives rejected by post-modernity, one that arises from
within ourselves and our experience – including what
Schillebeeckx has called our 'negative experience of contrast'.

Raymond Snoddy talks about a journalist William Stead who
worked in the 1880s on such issues as the improvement of slums
and the eradication of child prostitution. His difficulty lay in
pushing public figures to treat the issues urgently. He adopted
new techniques from the United States such as big black head-
lines and went along with 'sensationalism' up to the point necessary 'to arrest the eye of the public and compel them to admit
the necessity of action'. He goes on to the conclusion that
'Newspapers are at their best when they are not sticking their
noses into someone's private life but dealing with life and death
and justice.'[4]

The anecdote sits rather well alongside post-modernity's so-
called distrust of institutions. It invites the idea of the post-modern journalist as one with a strong sense of working 'for the sake
of' something – as somebody in whom a passion has been awak-
ened.

Discourse
I began by saying that 'discourse' means serious conversation.
In our cultural memory, the classic instance of discourse is the

---

4. *The Good, the Bad and the Unacceptable,* London, Faber & Faber, 1993,
47, 58.

dialogues of Plato, centred on the person of Socrates. The inter-play between Socrates and the Sophists in those dialogues stands almost as a symbol of the two strands noted in post-modern journalism.

Socrates is the lover of wisdom, committed to dialogue and to the truth that emerges from dialogue conducted in a spirit of deep mutual respect. In the *Gorgias* he says to Polus that he cares nothing for what the whole world thinks 'if only I may obtain your agreement'. He says to Polus, 'I have a high regard for you.' Later he addresses Callicles: 'I am simply your fellow ex-plorer in the search for truth.'

The Sophists, on the other hand, were educators become ora-tors. They possessed the techniques of communication and per-suasion, but without the spiritual awakening. Theirs, as Plato put it, was the skill of 'making the worse cause appear the bet-ter'. Socrates spoke of them when he remarked that 'It is quite possible to pander to the souls of a crowd, without regard to its real interest.' All this is strangely resonant with the 'game' and the 'play' in post-modernity. The style rather than the substance. Pandering instead of discourse. On the one hand, the dialogue as a loving search for truth; on the other, a playing with words, the post-modern *jouissance*.

'Moral discourse' is in an ambiguous place in post-modern culture. Today's journalism shares that experience of ambiguity. John Horgan captures the tension well as it manifests itself in the school of journalism:

> In Irish journalism education, no less, there is an unresolved, and perhaps irresolvable, tension between teaching students the codes they need to employ to produce the sort of accept-able news stories which will enable them to satisfy cautious media executives that they are employable, and the critical skills necessary to ensure that they can continue to exercise some of journalism's essential functions in a free society.[5]

From one angle, we can see journalism today as a forum where moral discourse is battling for its own identity. From another, we can see it as a forum where journalism is battling for its own identity as an essentially moral form of discourse.

---

5. *The Furrow*, February, 1995.

CHAPTER SIX

Contemporary humanitarianism: neutral and impartial?

Linda Hogan

One of the defining features of the post-Cold War world is the rise in the frequency and intensity of humanitarian interventions. Yet, although welcomed by many as a sign of global solidarity, humanitarian interventions continue to be controversial. The failed intervention in Somalia in 1992 prompted a strong reaction against humanitarian relief in conflict areas altogether. Yet subsequent inaction in Rwanda showed how non-intervention is also a questionable option.[1] True, the eventual 'success' in Kosovo has mitigated the effects of Somalia somewhat. However, the post-9/11 situation is more complicated still because of the contentious role that 'the humanitarian case for war' played in the interventions in both Afghanistan and Iraq. As a member-state of the United Nations and latterly of the European Union, Ireland has played a significant role in humanitarian interventions, both military and non-military. In addition, a myriad of Irish NGOs are involved in non-military operations that typically include electoral monitoring, refugee repatriation and the distribution of humanitarian relief supplies. Yet, to date there has not been much by way of ethical reflection from an Irish perspective on the nature of contemporary humanitarianism, in its military and non-military forms. Reflection on the issue of humanitarianism in light of Catholic moral principles is necessary too because of the myriad ways in which Catholics formally and informally are involved in the field. At a formal level, through its many national and international bodies, the church participates in public debate on this issue. Moreover, its teaching is often important for the many Catholics who hold political office and who are attentive to the principles of Catholic social thought in their work.

---

1. Although non-intervention is technically an inaccurate description of the international community's involvement in Rwanda, it is the general perception that the inadequate and tardy nature of that intervention meant that it was effectively equivalent to non-intervention.

As a global organisation the Catholic Church is also the sponsor of a significant proportion of the non-governmental aid world-wide. Large organisations like Catholic Relief Services (USA), Caritas Internationalis, Misereor, Cordaid, and Comité Contre la Faim et Pour le Developpement (CCFD), Trócaire and others have a major role in the provision of humanitarian aid. A Catholic social justice agenda is also promoted by the thousands of smaller Catholic charities and aid agencies that operate inter-nationally. Thus in the global humanitarian network the church plays a significant role, both in the provision of aid and in shap-ing the values that ground it. And since the values which ground humanitarianism are currently under dispute, it is es-sential that the church contribute to the discussion. It seems ap-propriate therefore, given our honorand's long-standing interest in social ethics, that this festschrift should provide the opportu-nity for an initial exploration of the topic.

In fact there has been a tremendous growth of academic liter-ature on humanitarian interventions in the past ten years, much of it discussing the legal and ethical basis on which state inter-vention might be legitimate. Legal arguments have tended to focus on interpretations of Chapter VII of the UN Charter, while ethical debates have been more wide-ranging.[2] Making substan-tial use of traditional just war doctrine, analyses of the ethics of humanitarian interventions have focused on questions that fit into the conventional categories of *jus ad bellum* and *jus in bello*. And although there are disagreements about the details, most academics advocate adopting a framework that requires the

----

2. Article 2 (7) of the UN Charter states that 'Nothing contained in the present Charter shall authorize the UN to intervene in matters which are essentially within the domestic jurisdiction of any State or shall re-quire the Members to submit such matters to settlement under the pre-sent Charter; but this principle shall not prejudice the application of en-forcement measures under Chapter VII.' Chapter VII then deals with action with respect to threats to the peace, breaches of the peace and acts of aggression and is the basis on which recent debates about inter-vention have taken place. However, there is a great deal of ambiguity here because Chapter VII does not mention humanitarian crises as the basis for intervention. Many commentators therefore argue that recent Security Council resolutions have made improper use of Chapter VII in the effort to legitimate interventions for humanitarian purposes. The humanitarian brief taken on by the Security Council in Resolution 688, April 5 1991 in respect of the Iraqi civilian population is a case in point.

presence of a just cause, intervention as a last resort, proportionality of means and probability of success in order for an intervention to be justified.[3] Yet there are limits to the usefulness of
reasoning analogously from just war principles. In particular the
question of the motivation introduces a significant point of difference, one which has not as yet had the scholarly attention it
deserves. Some in the realist school believe that self-interest is
the only legitimate basis on which one state should intervene in
the affairs of another, insisting that a state has a duty not to risk
the lives of its own civilian-soldiers in order to 'save strangers'.[4]
Yet according to the traditional definition of humanitarianism, it
is the interests of the target state and not those of the intervening
one that ought to be accorded primacy. Of course states rarely, if
ever, act for purely altruistic motives. And since states usually
have both political and humanitarian reasons for acting, the
ethical questions pertaining to motivation are complex. Indeed
the manner in which recent interventions have tended to elide
political and humanitarian concerns has led critics like Chomsky
to see in contemporary humanitarianism the revival of an earlier
imperialism, whose objective was to civilise. In his *New Military
Humanism: Lessons From Kosovo*, Chomsky criticises the Security
Council's acquiescence to NATO's determination to prosecute
the first 'humanitarian war', arguing that it exemplifies this
growing tendency to prosecute 'imperialistic wars under the
guise of humanitarian objectives'.[5] Throughout the conflict this
intertwining of political and humanitarian motivation was evident in statements by Prime Minister Blair, President Clinton and
a number of NATO generals. Clinton for example claimed 'we
are upholding our values, protecting our interests, and advanc-
ing the cause of peace' and claimed that had the USA faltered

3. See for example Wheeler, N., *Saving Strangers, Humanitarian Intervention in International Society*, OUP, 2000 and Ramsbotham, O. &
Woodhouse, T., *Humanitarian Intervention in Contemporary Conflict, A
Reconceptualisation*, Oxford, Polity Press, 1996 for extensive discussions
of the principles necessary for justified interventions.
4. See for example Mason, A. & Wheeler, N., 'Realist Objections to
Humanitarian Intervention', in Holden, B., (ed) *The Ethical Dimensions
of Global Change*, London, Macmillan, 1996 for a comprehensive discussion of this tradition in international relations. See also Condoleeza Rice
'Promoting the National Interest', *Foreign Affairs* 79, No 1 2000, 47.
5. Chomsky, N., *The New Military Humanism: Lessons From Kosovo*,
London, Pluto Press, 1999.

'the result would have been a moral and strategic disaster.'[6] Chomsky questions the reliability of the humanitarian motivations, pointing to the reluctance to prosecute a ground war as one example of the manner in which the self-interest of the superpowers dominated the agenda. However, beyond the ethics of this particular intervention, the central claim of Chomsky's book is that we are witnessing the development of a 'new military humanism' in which humanitarianism, along with globalisation, have become the new forms of western imperialism.

The phrase 'humanitarian intervention' can refer to a range of activities, from the work of NGOs on long-term projects in relatively stable developing countries, to military interventions to protect human rights in a war zone. And although the means of interventions vary greatly, they tend to share the objective of alleviating suffering, protecting against human rights abuses and building peace. In short, they seek to promote humanitarian outcomes in impoverished and often violent circumstances. However, the changed political context has raised some serious questions about the viability of the inherited model of humanitarianism, both in terms of its nature and in terms of its means. In relation to the means by which humanitarianism is pursued, an analysis of the growing militarisation of humanitarian interventions, exemplified in the oxymoron 'humanitarian war', is long overdue. However this cannot be pursued here.[7] Rather the focus of this essay will be on the adequacy of the traditional understanding of humanitarianism as apolitical and impartial. In particular we will consider whether the inherited model of humanitarianism is either sustainable or appropriate, given the new political context in which humanitarian interventions are contemplated today.

Humanitarianism: The Principle of Neutrality
Traditionally humanitarianism has been characterised by the four core principles of humanity, universality, impartiality and neutrality. These principles are the legacy of Jean Henri Dunant,

---

6. Chomsky, ibid., quoting articles from *Boston Globe* and *New York Times*.
7. This issue is discussed in 'The Case for the Abolition of War in the Twenty-First Century', written jointly by Stanley Hauerwas, Linda Hogan and Enda McDonagh, *Journal of the Society of Christian Ethics*, 2005 (2).

founder of International Committee of the Red Cross (ICRC), who in 1859 witnessed the horror of war at the battlefield of Solferino on which 38,000 men lay dead or wounded after fifteen hours of fighting. The principle of humanity recognises that a common humanity continues to exist behind all political divisions, and that it persists even in war. The principle of universality asserts an attachment to common values, in which all people share equal duties and responsibilities to help one another. Universality grounds the entire humanitarian enterprise since a shared commitment to certain values is the basis on which humanitarianism operates. However, the nature and reliability of these minimal values is intensely contested from many quarters today.[8] With impartiality the issue is non-discrimination in responding to need. This core value is enshrined in all four Geneva Conventions and requires that victims be protected without distinction based on race, colour, sex, language, religion or belief. Moreover need, and not any other consideration, is to be the determining factor in the provision of aid. The expectation that humanitarianism will be neutral, i.e. non-political, has been regarded as the defining principle of humanitarianism. Underlying this principle of neutrality is the assumption that it is possible to separate political and humanitarian concerns. However, even in the early years of the ICRC (which was the organisation that both articulated and best embodies this version of 'apolitical' humanitarianism) this construction of the nature of humanitarianism was disputed. Moreover it continues to be the most contested of the defining principles of humanitarianism. Some argue that humanitarian ends can only be achieved through politics, while others argue for separating them. But even more significant is the question of whether this kind of neutral, impartial humanitarianism is possible. Classically the ICRC regards its work as apolitical, yet it is based on consent from those with political power, who expect that there will be little or no overt criticism of the state's behaviour. This may be both necessary and ethical, its critics argue, but it is certainly not apolitical.

---

8. Debates about shared or universal values take many forms and are of concern in the fields of political philosophy, human rights theory as well as ethics. Although the substance of the debate is beyond the scope of this paper, it does have significant implications for the future of humanitarianism. Yet the debates about universal values and discussions about humanitarianism have, to date, proceeded on parallel lines.

This principle of neutrality at the core of humanitarianism has thus long been the subject of debate. Indeed the ICRC has been the catalyst for this because of its determination to hold on to this version of humanitarianism in light of serious criticisms of certain of its activities. Some of its work during World War II has been particularly controversial, with many regarding the organisation as having failed in its duty to victims because of its decision to stay silent on the issue of the work and death camps in Europe. The ICRC itself has endlessly debated this difficult issue of neutrality (which is exemplified in the question of whether the organisation should speak out or remain silent in the face of atrocities), as is evident from Caroline Moorehead's[9] analysis of the internal arguments that occurred within the organisation at that time. Aware of the ambiguous effects, as well as the difficulties it places on its staff, the ICRC's consistent position nonetheless has been to preserve confidentiality and avoid condemnation in the fulfilment of its 'exclusive mission' which is 'to protect the lives and dignity of victims of war and internal violence and to provide them with assistance'.[10] In reflecting on the issue of whether the ICRC should choose condemnation or silence in the face of knowledge of atrocities (which it characterises as a choice between politics or neutrality), the ICRC President Dr Jakob Kellenberger defended the organisation's traditional position of using the knowledge it acquires through its activity exclusively for its humanitarian activity.[11] In order to further reinforce this position, Kellenberger described one ICRC staff member's statement on May 17 2001 that Israel's settlements in the Occupied Territories amount to a war crime as a mistake. Although hailed in many circles as an indication that the ICRC had given up what critics regard as 'its naïve apoliticism', the ICRC at the official level regards this statement as regrettable.[12] Moreover it has maintained this position even in the face of criticism of its refusal to give evidence to the International Criminal Tribunal for the Former Yugoslavia or to the International Criminal Tribunal for Rwanda.

9. Moorehead, C., *Dunant's Dream, War, Switzerland and the History of the Red Cross*, London, HarperCollins, 1998.
10. ICRC Mission Statement available at http://www.icrc.org
11. Kellenberger, J., 'Reflections on Speaking Out or Remaining Silent in Humanitarian Activity', delivered in Zürich 27 June 2001 available at http://www.icrc.org
12. Ibid.

Taking the lead from the ICRC many NGOs, including Catholic NGOs, explicitly adopted this approach to humanitarianism. Particularly in the early decades of their activity, when Catholic development agencies were concerned primarily with relief, the neutrality of their humanitarian activity was uncontested. Today, however, because of the changed political landscape in which emergencies arise, the posture of neutrality is more difficult to sustain. In particular today humanitarian interventions often take place in highly volatile conflict situations and this changed context inevitably alters its nature. Since most of the emergencies of the last decade have taken place in warzones, or in 'collapsing' states (as for example in Somalia) relief agencies have relied on military forces to create a humanitarian space within which they can operate. This necessarily involves a more complex intertwining of political and humanitarian spaces and raises questions for NGOs about their ability to maintain their traditional posture of neutrality. The lead story on *The Sunday Times* of 4 November 2001, exemplifies this problem. In the early weeks of what was variously described as a 'war on terror' or a 'war of self-defence' the incursion of US and UK armies into Afghanistan was described in this way: 'American and British forces are about to mount the first significant ground offensive of the war in Afghanistan in an attempt to establish a "humanitarian bridgehead", that would bring winter relief to hundreds of thousands of refugees.' It is interesting to note the tension between the description of the operation itself, i.e. 'the first significant ground offensive of the war' with the newly stated objective, i.e. 'to establish a 'humanitarian bridgehead'. Indeed the public relations machinery of both governments had been at pains to point out the 'good humanitarian reasons' to oust the Taliban. However, the repressive regime of the Taliban notwithstanding, many regarded this move as a cynical and opportunistic use of a very grave humanitarian crisis in the attempt to legitimate a war waged for different reasons.[13] The failure of the international community to act in support of the civilian population in Afghanistan earlier despite the fact that already in 1996 it ranked 170 out of 174 on the UN Index of Human Development

---

13. This comment does not imply a judgement about the legitimacy or not of the political reasons for waging a war against Afghanistan, the criticism relates to using a humanitarian emergency to cloak political interests.

fuels this suspicion of opportunism. The example of Afghanistan serves here merely to highlight the growing difficulty of
maintaining the separation of the political and the humanitarian
aspects of relief. In particular this trend poses significant problems for humanitarian agencies that increasingly need the support of armed forces to create the space in which aid can be delivered. Difficulties arise for agencies, including Catholic ones,
when they are associated in the minds of the target populations,
with an unwelcome or even aggressive military force. The deliv-
ery of humanitarian aid frequently involves negotiations with
local militias as well as the protection of UN or other non-in-
digenous forces that are often regarded as partisan. Thus even
when agencies wish to affirm their neutrality, the political situation may make this virtually impossible. The very public debate
between a British army commander of forces in Afghanistan and
a representative from CAFOD (Catholic Agency for Overseas
Development) in the autumn of 2001 captures this difficulty.
During a debate on BBC Radio 4 the CAFOD worker expressed
the concern that CAFOD and other relief agencies had, that their
impartial and humanitarian relief was being used by the US and
British governments as one of the arms of the war machine. Yet
the nature of the conflicts in many of the contemporary crisis
zones means that this relationship between the military and the
humanitarian agencies will continue to be intertwined. Indeed
the dilemma for humanitarian agencies is just one manifestation
of the manner in which, at all levels, humanitarian and politico-
military mandates are becoming more interconnected.

Humanitarianism: The Principle of Impartiality
The changed political context in which humanitarianism is pursued today raises questions about the adequacy of these traditional values of neutrality and impartiality. However, the need
for a more explicitly political form of humanitarianism is also
being advocated by NGOs (including Catholic ones) and governments who believe that humanitarian assistance should always be linked to interventions that promote human rights and
conflict resolution.[14] In the background too is a frequently articulated concern that occasionally the provision of aid can serve to
prolong and intensify conflict. Interventions in Zaire, Sierra

14. See Shawcross, W., *Deliver Us From Evil, Peacekeepers Warlords and a
World of Endless Conflict*, New York, Simon & Schuster, 2000.

Leone, Sudan and Kosovo serve as examples of this new trend towards conditionality in humanitarian aid, with assistance delivered or withheld on the basis of political, and not exclusively humanitarian, principles. The articulation of this explicitly 'political humanitarianism' can be linked to the founding of *Medecins sans Frontieres* (MSF) in 1971 by Bernard Kouchner. An ICRC doctor at the time, Kouchner was frustrated by the apoliticism of that organisation during the Biafran war and founded MSF, an organisation that, in his own words, 'was political from the start'.[15] Accepting the Nobel Peace Prize on behalf of the organisation in 1999 he went on to say that he hoped the prize 'marks the recognition of a type of humanitarian work which fights injustice and persecution, in contrast to traditional organisations.'[16] MFS's President, Phillipe Biberson, reinforced the point with what appeared to be a concealed reference to the ICRC, by claiming 'we are not sure that speaking out always saves lives, but we are certain that silence kills'.[17] It is interesting to note here that the twentieth century opened with the Nobel Peace Prize being awarded to the ICRC and ended with it being awarded to its most vociferous critic MSF. Each symbolises a different approach to the orientation of humanitarianism *vis-à-vis* politics. But far from being simply a dispute between two rival organisations, this debate is significant for the future shape of humanitarian work, both at the governmental and non-governmental levels.

The outcome of the debate about aid to refugee camps populated by Rwandans in Zaire between 1994 and 1996 provides an interesting example of the triumph of 'political' over 'neutral' humanitarianism and raises some troubling ethical issues, particularly from a Christian perspective. The flight of Hutus from Rwanda fearing retribution following two years of genocide led to a heated debate among aid agencies, including Catholic ones, regarding the provision of aid to the camps in which the refugees settled. In a media debate that raged for two years, aid agencies were accused of feeding the perpetrators of the genocide in Rwanda.[18] There is no doubt that, among the refugees in

15. Fox, F., *The Politicisation of Aid*, unpublished paper, please do not quote.
16. Ibid., 9.
17. Ibid., 9
18. There were similar anxieties during the famine relief operation in Somalia in 1991, although that did not result in the mass exodus of aid agencies from the region.

Zaire, were individuals who were subsequently charged with serious crimes. For those like Alex de Waal who advocate what he calls an 'ethical' humanitarianism, the work of aid agencies in the region embodied the worst aspects of neutral or apolitical relief. Many commentators argued that aid agencies were indirectly supporting a genocidal Hutu regime, providing the resources to allow former Hutu military to re-arm, strengthen their resources and prepare for assault on the Tutsi regime. Such was the clamour in the media, which reported the presence of former Hutu militia in the refugee camps endlessly, that most relief agencies withdrew, rather than face the moralising wrath of the international media. Thus 'within a year of the refugees arriving in Goma the number of relief agencies operating in the refugee camps had dropped from 150 to 5.'[19] Eventually the camps were closed and the UNHCR was involved in what many regarded as the involuntary repatriation of refugees to Rwanda. Clare Short, the UK minister responsible for development and humanitarian affairs at the time, and who is a strong advocate of this new 'ethical' humanitarianism, analysed the situation thus: 'In the case of Rwanda, following the genocide, the people who led the genocide then led the refugees out of the country, the cameras went in, all the resources were piled in and they were delivered through those who had organised the genocide and they were massively strengthened ... So humanitarian assistance strengthened the evil forces which had brought about the genocide in Rwanda.'[20] Yet the former Head of Emergencies at a major international aid agency described what happened in Zaire as 'a new low for humanitarian principles' in which the most depressing aspect has been the willingness of ... 'the UN and NGO humanitarian relief agencies and donors, to abandon international humanitarian law in the face of political imperatives.'[21] It is clear therefore that what its advocates describe as a 'more political or ethical humanitarianism' has the potential to undermine the principles of neutrality and impartiality that are at the heart of traditional humanitarianism. Moreover it runs the risk of dividing victims into deserving and undeserving and may result in

19. Ibid., 23.
20. Clare Short in evidence to the IDC cited in Fox, op. cit., 23.
21. James Fennell, 'Hope Suspended: Morality, Politics and War in Central Africa', *RRN Newsletter*, November 1997 quoted in Fox, F., op. cit., 24.

the lives of certain individuals being sacrificed in the pursuit of an, albeit admirable, long-term goal.

The refugee crisis in Zaire crystallised the already simmering conflict between 'neutral' and 'principled' humanitarianism. In the years that have followed many of the key actors, including OECD, the EU, the IMF and the World Bank have begun to promote conditional aid and principled (read political) humanitarianism. The British government too has been a champion of this development, and one can also see its influence in the justice and human rights approach increasingly being favoured by Catholic development agencies.[22] It is important to note, however, that, although unease about the destination of some aid has been an obvious catalyst for the articulation of a principled humanitarianism, the rationale for such a development has a more substantial basis in the belief that the long-term efficacy of aid is best assured by the promotion of certain political agendas. Indeed this fits with a more general move away from unconditional aid, towards a vision of sustainable development in which the provision of external aid is one aspect of a strategy to deal with the underlying causes of the particular emergency. Summarising this approach Peter Uvin says: 'There clearly is a broad trend towards an increased use of humanitarian assistance as part of a more comprehensive strategy to transform conflicts and decrease the violence.'[23] One can see the effects of this in the fact that many aid agencies have adjusted their primary focus in the past two decades and now concentrate on long-term, politically engaged programmes that seek to address the underlying causes of suffering and that work to promote justice and conflict-resolution. Catholic NGOs too have been affected by this development, and many have adopted more long-term, justice-based strategies in their development work. No doubt there is much to be commended in this approach. However, what it means for the neutrality and impartiality of the humanitarianism that these agencies have traditionally embodied has yet to be properly considered.

The church's humanitarian work is grounded in a belief in the inherent dignity and worth of each human being. Speaking

---

22. This comment is based on personal knowledge of a number of Catholic development agencies, but has not yet been properly verified.
23. Uvin, P., 'The Influence of Aid in Situations of Violent Conflict', *OECD Report*, September 1999, in Fox, 10.

on the 50th anniversary of the Geneva Conventions in 1999, Pope John Paul II drew attention to this when he commented that 'Minimum protection of the dignity of every person, guaranteed by international humanitarian law, is all too often violated in the name of military or political demands which should never prevail over the value of the person. Today we are aware of the need to find a new consensus on humanitarian principles and to reinforce their foundations to prevent the recurrence of atrocities and abuse. The church never tires of ... actively working with those who strive to assure aid to the suffering, and to ensure respect for their dignity ... whether they are civilians or military.'[24] The cases discussed in this essay highlight the dilemmas created by this demand that we attend to the dignity of each person. Moreover the cases also suggest that the imperatives of building a sustainable peace can result in the well-being of individuals and groups being ignored or sacrificed, thereby making Pope John Paul II's call for a new consensus on humanitarian principles all the more urgent.

There are undoubtedly resources within the church's own tradition of social thought on which we can draw when trying to unravel the complex demands of humanitarian work today. The fact that, from the beginning, this tradition has preserved the two inter-related discourses of love and justice may suggest a way of proceeding. Indeed the endurance of the twin discourses of love and justice through the centuries indicates that they both have a significant role to play as the church articulates its own distinctive response to inequality and oppression. Yet to date we have not given much attention to the significance of the presence of these two distinctive modes of social engagement or their inter-relation. Solidarity with all human beings, care for even the perpetrators of appalling acts of violence, together with the promotion of justice and the defence of human rights, all combine to suggest a Christian social ethic of extraordinary complexity. And it is surely in the nuances of this tradition that the church will find the resources that will help it to resolve these seemingly intractable dilemmas as the world moves, inexorably, or so it seems, from neutral to political humanitarianism.

---

24. Pope John Paul II, General Audience, on the 50th Anniversary of the Geneva Conventions, 11 August 1999.

CHAPTER SEVEN

On having a religious morality

Vincent MacNamara

Recent statements from church and state suggest that a new consideration of the relations between the two is timely.[1] There is a recognition that the situation has changed. Two things in particular may be adverted to. The secularisation that Europe has known for quite some time is most decidedly among us. We are also beginning to experience a multi-cultural society. With different cultures come different religions, often inextricably entwined in the culture. And with different cultures/religions come different conceptions of morality. Churches that for centuries held sway here find their turf occupied by a multiplicity of faiths, some Christian, some not, but each with its own tradition and practices and discipline and dearly held beliefs.

Since the Enlightenment, the secular state has cast a jaundiced eye on Christian claims in the matter of morality and public policy. That, of course, continues. We hear more of it now in the European context, often in the form of a tension set up between what are referred to as religious viewpoints, facilely regarded as obscurantist, and the advance of science. Today the tension extends to the deeply held values, moral habits and religious symbols not only of Christianity but of the several religions which form a large part of the population. And there is tension between the different religious perspectives themselves. Fundamental – and particularly Western – moral and legal concepts of rights, freedom and conscience are involved, as well as more general notions of individualism, community, democracy, tradition, family. Where we might be going and what the tensions of the future might be, we can see from countries that have had a longer exposure to such developments.

So what will the new context require in the relationship of church, state and society? The relationship of church and state in

1. I refer to recent remarks by the Taoiseach and the Archbishop of Dublin.

Ireland, while it had different elements, has been most contro-
versially around issues of morality. At any moment in a debate
the Mother and Child scheme will surface. Or more or less recent
issues of abortion, contraception, divorce, assisted reproduction
of various kinds, homosexual acts, recognition of gay marriage,
the position of women, and the church response to child sexual
abuse. One suspects that many of those who are angry with the
church and who alight with glee on shortcomings on its part are
people who have felt victimised in their personal lives by state
regulations which, they felt, owed their provenance to church
influence or to church power. If you needed a civil divorce, for
example, and could not, until recently, get one, it was hard not
to feel that the culprit was ultimately the church.

The issue of church and state is a subject to which Patrick
Hannon has made and continues to make a notable contribution. I am not going to pursue that debate. But I offer some reflections on a question that lies behind it. That is: what does it
mean to do morality as a religious person or a religious institution? Which involves asking: what is the logic of and the justification for religious moral-language and what problems does it
create? That spins off into the questions: how might any religion
situate its moral claims in a multicultural, multi-religious state;
what are the possibilities for dialogue with moral traditions
other than one's own; what are the implications for a state or
community that has a multitude of religious moralities?

Religion: Morality
It may be that we do not appreciate the implications of that con-
junction of words 'religious morality', of which 'Christian
morality', 'Jewish morality', 'Muslim morality', 'Hindu morality'
are a subset. And perhaps that is because we do not give full
weight to the religious dimension. Religion and morality are
formally distinct. They deal with different clusters of questions.
It is, of course, perfectly possible for an explicitly non-religious
person to be sensitively moral. That is taken for granted. But
when we bring together these two profound strands of human
experience – the religious and the moral – we can expect
complications, various kinds of interdependence or interaction.
So let us look at the two strands.

It has been said that the most embarrassing thing about the
study of religion is the elusiveness of its subject-matter, but here

are some suggestions. 'Religion is the symbol that provides a "total" world interpretation, the myth that relates people to the ultimate conditions of their existence.'[2] 'Sacred symbols function to synthesise a people's ethos ...their worldview ... the picture they have of the way things in sheer actuality are, their most comprehensive ideas of order.'[3] The central issue is that of ultimacy: religion gives us our ultimate, all-encompassing view of life. Because it does so, it has its influence on culture, values and morals – it has often been remarked that it is impossible to separate religion and culture and we do not have to go beyond our own debate about whether the conflict in Northern Ireland was one of religion or culture.

We do not fare much better with attempts to find definitions of morality that are broad enough to include the diversity of moral models but specific enough to distinguish morality from other cultural expressions such as law, art, religion. It is widely agreed in Western philosophy that we are talking about a system that is prescriptive, that is authoritative, that is other-regarding, that is concerned with human welfare – but there will be disagreement about whether it deals with personal growth, with ideals, and whether or not it can be regarded as overriding with respect to other considerations etc. Indeed, as we shall see, it is such Western attempts of definition that are part of the problem for religious morality.

A Religious Morality
There are many ways in which behaviour is woven into religious experience or tradition. So there are different forms of dependence – epistemic, motivational, obligational, metaphysical, or dependence of content. One might ask of any religion about the very notion and source of morality and moral obligation with which it functions, or about the interpretation and significance of the whole moral enterprise and its relation to salvation. One will most obviously ask about the content of the moral code, about the kind of behaviour that is considered appropriate in the religion, and whether and how it is shaped or coloured by the religious strand.

2. Gregory Baum, 'Definitions of Religion in Sociology', *Concilium* 136 (1980), 27.
3. Clifford Geertz, 'Religion as a Cultural System', in D. Cutler, *The Religious Situation*, Boston, Beacon Press, 1968, 668.

The moral paradigm for the modern secular state is an Enlightenment version of a common or universal morality that is required by the structure of human reason. This non-historical, non-culturally mediated basis for morality is regarded as understandable by every liberated and right-thinking person and is to stand in judgement on every traditional form of morality. The problem is that many in society claim a superior moral knowledge derived from a religious system, and they dismiss as misguided or at least inadequate any other moral code. Their first loyalty, they believe, is to the wisdom of their religious heritage. The appeal is to God's word or God's promise or religious custom or a holy book or a representative of God, a prophet or teacher, to justify a particular piece of behaviour. So there is a struggle between religious obedience and what is proposed as 'rational' thought

It sometimes appears as a question about which is ultimate – moral experience or religious faith. Which wins out? Some have argued that moral considerations are, for the one who cares for them, the most important of all considerations and cannot be put aside for considerations of another kind. But we might wonder about that. Religious people might well ask why they should seek or settle for a common morality and might regard it as a betrayal, a wilful neglect of the truth. But that leaves us with a crucial question: can religion and its dictates overrule innate moral awareness? It has long been a concern of the secular tradition to protect morality from the vagaries of religion. But, on the other hand, religious adherents have doubted whether they should even allow the moral question to emerge as a rational question. We remember Kierkegaard's admiration of Abraham as a knight of faith and Barth's injunction that the grace of God protests against all man-made ethics so that there can be no armistice with the people of Canaan and their *cultus* and culture.[4] That suggests that one need not, indeed ought not, to doubt if one is doing what religious faith dictates.

A form of this is the often unstated belief that what is good for religious truth is good for the world. There are endless painful examples – justifications for the burning of heretics in the name of true religion, forced conversion, religious wars, military conquest of a religious kind, the 'Deus vult of the armed throng' (Chesterton's phrase) of the Crusades, 'The Lord is our

---

4. Karl Barth, *Church Dogmatics*, Edinburgh, Clark, 1957, II/2, 517, 524.

strength' of the Roundhead, appeals to scriptures in South
Africa and the Middle East, reprehensible church silence in the
face of evil. I read that Mohammed Atta, the chief of the Twin
Towers destroyers, asked in his will that his family should act
according to the example of Abraham, who, as a good Muslim,
offered his son to die.[5] Was his act a great act of religion?

Or can one discriminate among religions, good and bad: are
they to be judged by a moral criterion? It is a delicate question,
particularly in the light of expectations that freedom of religious
practice is sacred. 'Can all means be hallowed by religious ends?'
Küng asks. 'Is everything allowed in the service of religious de-
votion – even the misuse of economic and political power,
human sexuality or aggressiveness? May what appears inhuman,
what manifestly damages, violates, perhaps even destroys people,
be a religious commandment?'[6] I think the instinctive answer is
'No'. We do apply an ethical criterion. We trust the elemental significance of our moral sense and reject a deity or system that does
not respect human well-being at least in broadest terms. That still
leaves considerable space for differences of religious myth and of
practices that are congruent with them.

There are stronger and weaker forms of the dependence of
morality on religion. The stronger form is a divine command
theory of ethics. The weaker is not an epistemic dependence of
that kind but rather one of context and content. This suggests
that religions, even if they reject a notion of a direct revelation of
morality, are likely to have a characteristic morality, which will
differ from that of a different religious point of view and from a
non-religious point of view. The reason being that religion so
fundamentally affects one's view of life, of the world, of the person, of death, of the cosmos, of the future, of causality, of human
possibilities, that it is bound to affect one's moral positions – issues of freedom, welfare, harm, human dignity, truth, life, justice, wholeness, success etc., which are the common coin of the
moralist.

Many in the religions have been unapologetic about this.
Modernity rejected the whole notion of religious tradition and
authority. It saw religion as precisely the problem, with its

5. Francis Wheen, *How Mumbo Jumbo Conquered the World*, London,
Harper, 2004,165.
6. Hans Küng, *Global Responsibility: In Search of a New World Ethic*, trs
John Bowden, London, SCM, 1991, 83.

quixotic and particularist moral positions, which prevent rational agreement in society. (The multiplicity of religious views
and their disagreement is, of course, a godsend for this view.)
The fact that discussion about a common morality among non-
religious thinkers is an untidy mess is hardly adverted to. But
the reaction to modernity, and interestingly the thrust of post-
modernity, with its utter celebration of difference and diversity
and its assault on notions of a common human nature and a universal rationality, has had the interesting effect of giving a new
lease of life to the contextual nature of all ethics and as a consequence to religious ethics. Whether that is something that is to
be welcomed by religious ethics will be a matter of opinion.
There has long been a debate in Catholic circles about whether
there is a specific Christian morality. It seems more to the point
that all religions have a distinctive or characteristic morality. If
so, is it possible for them and for secular traditions to have a useful discussion about morality and come to agreements? Can one
ethical system talk to, clarify, learn from or judge another? Is
there at least a common logic of religious ethics, can one study
the manner in which the religious element affects the ethical –
allowing for the fact that adherents differ among themselves on
what is genuine Muslim or Christian ethics etc? In some sense
all religious moralities are contextual. The question is: how radical is this; and what are the implications for agreement, especially
in the area of public policy? This kind of study is important not
only for dialogue but in order to understand the logic of one's
own morality.

Comparative Studies
But the study tends to emphasise the differences rather than the
similarities. Comparative religious ethics involves different
kinds of comparison. Most obviously one will be interested in
the substantive issue of different content or moral code. But that
is likely to modify itself into questions about the manner of ethical justification, about how a religion justifies a particular code.
And deeper questions arise of a metaethical kind – particularly
in relation to a religion's range of myth. The concept of the deity,
if there be a deity, will be significant: is the deity concerned or
indifferent, benign or capricious, with a care for the well-being
of humans or 'careless of mankind'? There is the added problem
that it is often difficult to tease out different kinds of action

guide and to say whether or not they belong to the domain of morality. Notions of morality may not have become culturally explicit, still less the notion of ethics: 'we do this because our fathers and mothers did this'; 'we always did it this way', 'this is what our holy books prescribe'. So there will be difference not only about what is right and wrong but about what counts as morality, what counts as justification, and most basically about the worldview from which viewpoints emerge. In any work of dialogue there is an ever-present danger of applying one's own prejudices, even one's conception of rationality: there is often the unconscious assumption that terms and categories that are valid in one context are equally valid in a radically different culture.

Nonetheless, in this kind of comparative work some will claim to find similarities but will differ about what kind of similarity. Some claim congruence of a substantive kind, because they are convinced of a Kantian universalist structure of rationality – a mode of reasoning common to all human beings. This would expect to discover actual commonalities, concrete norms. It cannot imagine values or virtues that would be compelling only in the context of a specific way of life. Others seek the similarities not so much in concrete norms as in a possible thread of rationality in systems that have different views about the nature of non-moral reality. They acknowledge differences but they claim to find a basic religious and moral logic, a form of deduction from an overall worldview that can help explain seeming inconsistencies and that can facilitate dialogue.

Still others take their stand on some notion of a common human nature and common human needs. They point to spheres of human experience that figure in more or less any human life and in which more or less any human being will have to make some choices rather than others, and act in some way rather than some other. So, for example, with regard to justice or compassion or respect, people disagree about what it means in practice to be just or compassionate or respectful but what they are arguing about is the most appropriate way to act with regard to this sphere. So, different cultural accounts are seen not as untranslateably different but as competing accounts about a set of shared human experiences. This allows one to compare traditions. Just how far it gets you is something we must come back to.

Contextual Dependence

But many now doubt the utility of applying conventional Western philosophical concepts – definitions of 'religion' and 'ethics' and 'rationality' and 'justification' and 'well-being' – in the search for significant agreement. They make the point that we are led back to an approach that treats a system of beliefs as a whole and refuses to isolate moral propositions or practices from propositions or stories about how things are in the world and how they came to be that way. One has to take the whole web of beliefs, the inner perspective and dynamic of the great religions with their own kind of consistency. How one ought to act and what one ought to be – one's outlook regarding the nature of morality, of the good, of relationships to other humans, to matter, to the cosmos – is related in one way or another to one's view of what life is all about, to one's ultimate framework of existence. Cosmogony will guide choice. The obverse is also true: strong convictions about a particular action will send one in search of the cosmogony in which that action makes sense.

This view is not sanguine about any universal account of practical reason or about anything but a thin account of basic features of human life and its claims. Its thesis is that people with different religio-moral languages live in different moral worlds, not definable in the terms of other forms of moral understanding. Religious myth, ethical claim, and the way of life together form a coherent whole but how these connect with one another will differ from culture to culture. Their inner logic is specific to themselves. Practical reason itself is tradition bound. So that what looks like agreement about justice or rights or fairness or honesty will be deceptively formal and may be disappointing in the concrete. We have recently seen philosophical versions of this view insist that the very terms that need to be deconstructed are 'freedom', 'justice', 'individuality', 'autonomy', 'democracy', 'community', 'enemy', 'war'. Facile claims for universals are to be treated with caution.

The experience of Alan Donagan is instructive. He famously stated that Hebrew-Christian morality was simply a matter of pure practical reason. Which left him in the position of saying that moralities that disagreed with this, e.g. Hinduism, were either deficient in practical reason or inept at exercising it. That in the end was unacceptable, so that he had to come to the now well-known conclusion: 'The moral tradition associated with the

Jewish and Christian religions is incompatible in various respects with other venerable moral traditions, for example that of
Hinduism.' The notions of tradition and worldview are therefore essential to the explanation of moral disagreement: what
matters is 'what is distinctive in the presuppositions of the
Hebrew-Christian tradition about the nature of human beings
and their world'.[7] There are critical issues embedded here: because it is fundamental to the doing of ethics, as Western philosophy understands it – and here it will differ from Hinduism –
that we are involved with questions whether and to what extent
we are free agents or objects of determination from without,
whether and in what ways we are related to one another, to non
human realities, to transcendence, and what implications these
statements of relatedness hold.

Contextual dependence, as we shall see, is directly at odds
with the official Catholic position. But some other Christians en-
dorse it. They acknowledge that their Christian tradition, with
its language and culture, provides a framework that shapes the
way those who have learned it perceive reality and order their
lives. As they see it, to belong to a religious community is never
incidental to our self-understanding. In this perspective what
Christians have is an internal realism, an internal community
cogency. The truth of Christian moral claims, like the claims of
any other religious morality, can only be established internal to
its beliefs and therefore requires a facility with its language and
its entire worldview. This tends not to be a foundationalist position in which a whole fan of truths can be articulated from one
primordial principle. What you have here is a kind of bricolage
of relevant Christian elements.

It is this, I take it, that is in question when one uses that vague
word 'ethos'. It is a valid notion. It rests on the fact that worldview colours the perception of behaviour. At its best, the
Christian tradition, for example, suggests and encourages behaviour that is characterised by trust and hope in God, care for
each individual, acceptance of the goodness of creation, appreciation of life, simplicity, forgiveness, tolerance, a distinctive valu-
ation of goods. If there is such a thing as a distinctive Christian
morality this is the justification and source of it. But these are
general orientations. It is possible that Christians will disagree

7. Alan Donagan, *The Theory of Morality*, Chicago, University of Chicago
Press, 1977, xv, 33-35.

about the weight to be given to different aspects of the ethos. They may come to different conclusions. It may also be that patience, tolerance, a recognition of the importance of and the reason for difference, and a concern for the sincerely held viewpoint of others, which are elements of the ethos, will make one hesitant about pushing one's own firm convictions in society. Ethos naturally issues in a style of life but it does not easily or automatically translate into rules. To take a critical example, many Christians assent to and live a commitment to the goodness of life and procreation without assenting to the proposition that every act of intercourse must be open to procreation.

The contextual approach brings us to this point. To a distinction of justification and truth. Claims will be justified contextually. They depend on the worldview of the community which makes them. 'There is no sphere of morality independent of the agent's metaphysical or theological (or anti-theological) view of the world and more particularly of God and the self.'[8] 'You cannot somehow leap out of culture and history altogether and gaze directly into the Moral Law.'[9] The starting point here is that moralities retain their intelligibility only within the traditions that articulate them: this then calls for a historical, local, inwardly coherent understanding of different systems. Whether or not claims are true is a different matter. Truth is something to be discovered patiently and through dialogue.

Such a plethora of religio-moral positions leads to the frustration of those who believe they have outgrown religion and to the strictures of philosophers like Frankena. 'If morality is dependent on religion, then we cannot hope to solve our problems or resolve our differences of opinion about them, unless and insofar as we can achieve agreement and certainty in religion (not a lively hope).'[10] His concern is to establish the independence of moral discourse from all the relativities of human interests and commitments save one – the interest of being rational. But the

---

8. Alasdair MacIntyre, 'Moral Philosophy:What Next?', in Alasdair MacIntyre and Stanley Hauerwas, *Revisions*, Indiana, Notre Dame Press, 1983, 14.
9. Jeffrey Stout, *Ethics After Babel*, Cambridge, James Clarke and Co, 1990, 23
10. William K. Frankena, 'Is Morality Logically Dependent on Religion?' in Gene Outka and John P.Reeder Jr., *Religion and Morality*, New York, Anchor, 1973, 296.

notion of 'the rational' was always a matter of obscurity. As it is used here, it assumes that if religious commitments are knocked away pure shining truth will emerge. But pure rationality is a chimera. It is hard to see that any construal of the human is free from presuppositions, and that is bound to affect moral judgement. It is a massive assumption that the non-religious point of view is the one most likely to yield the truth about living. No one argues in a vacuum. The Enlightenment idea of rationality has suffered its own disparagement from the invective of Postmodernism. The ideal is not an either/or: either the Enlightenment model based on a rational nature available to all rightthinking people or a ghetto morality of religious groups.

What of Natural Law?
In the light of all this, the position of Catholic moral teaching is particularly interesting. On the face of it, this appears to be strongly universalist. One must not forget its rich tradition of virtue and ideal. But its basic position is that the great lines of morality are available to people generally without the aid of explicit revelation – but that in order to understand the moral way 'easily, with certainty and without admixture of error', 'given the present sate of fallen nature' (*Dei Verbum* 6), one needs religious revelation. It claims that what can be arrived at by reason and what is revealed is the 'rational order', the fullness of the natural law universally understandable and communicable. So it sees its teaching as valid for all peoples and all times. Hence the rejection of relativism and short shrift for considerations raised about the influence of culture. The magisterium has persistently clung to this version of natural law (even if it has departed somewhat from a rigidly biological view of nature). But many theologians have long since found untenable its classicist position on nature and its failure to take account of history and culture.[11]

The appeal to biblical texts, what the documents call 'revealed moral truths', which will copperfasten natural argument, occurs explicitly in most of the documents. The appeal in *Humanae Vitae*, however, is different – not an appeal to specific texts but 'a teaching founded on the natural law, illuminated and enriched by divine Revelation'. This seems to be the

11. See especially *Veritatis Splendor*, 36, 58-50, 78-88, *Persona Humana*, 3-5, *Evangelium Vitae*, 113, 137.

methodology also in other areas: in the argument that life is a
gift of God used in condemnations of murder; in the argument
that the goods of the earth are meant by God to be shared by all
in teachings on justice and property. Does it operate in the matter of abortion? The argument here is, on the face of it and perhaps essentially, a moral, not a religious argument and can be
advanced solely as a moral argument. *Evangelium Vitae* ac-
knowledges that scripture does not address the question of direct abortion. But its argument is shaped by reference to the
great respect required by the divine commandment, 'you shall
not kill', by reference to the fact that all human beings, from
their mother's womb, belong to God who searches them and
knows them and whose vocation is even now written in the
'book of life', by its insistence that from its very beginning
human life directly involves God's creative activity.[12] Is it a religious background about God as creator and about the goodness
of life that colours the Catholic position?

   It might be useful to note two points here. The first concerns
moral argument. For a variety of reasons, it is often not easy to
arrive at moral conclusions. Background, temperament and
philosophical worldview influence judgment – in the reading of
facts, in the weighing of values, in the judgement of proportion,
in the assessment of consequences, in the weight of circumstances. One person's rationality is another's naïveté. Many factors, often unconscious, go into the arriving at a specific point of
view. It is likely that one's religious viewpoint will be of subtle
significance. The second point is that such a looser, more
imaginative, more community-influenced use of scripture is just
what scripture scholars are recommending to moralists, rather
than an explicit and direct dependence on texts.

   What part then do religious considerations play in these arguments? Is one led to posit a Catholic natural law? Is it the case
that its positions on life, procreation, experimentation, cloning,
same-sex unions, homosexuality, abortion, marriage, divorce,
justice – to take a number of crucial cases – are dependent on or
influenced by its religious view of the world? The appeal here is
not to texts of the Bible, but to something that one might call the
general values of the Bible – less precise than rules – or 'a
Catholic ethos' – less precise again. They are intelligible and de-
fensible concepts. But is this where the block occurs when the

---

12. See especially *Humanae Vitae* 4, *Evangelium Vitae*, 94-95, 61-62.

magisterium finds itself at odds with reasonable people who do not share its religious background?

We are back to the contextual nature of judgements, although the magisterium steadfastly sets its face against that. What seems to be in question here is human nature understood in a theological base. It is a construal of nature according to which some aspects of that nature are given great normative weight, while others are de-emphasised. Such a conception of natural law does not offer a morality that is universally convincing. This does not mean that its positions are not wise or humanly best. Nor does it mean that they will not be shared by other religions and some non-religious. They are far from being eccentric. There is nothing very eccentric about belief in and commitment, at least in broad terms, to the goodness of creation, of life and of human community: such orientations offer at least an important starting point for dialogue. But it does mean that Catholics need to recognise that these viewpoints, and particularly concrete norms too sharply drawn from them, will not necessarily commend themselves to other sincere seekers of the truth. It is not a matter of a failure of intelligence or of diligence, but of difference of perspective.[13]

Agreement in Morals
Even an unrelenting contextualist outlook does not mean that there cannot be dialogue – provided one can enter into the complex web of another tradition's logic. Except in the extreme view, it does not mean a hard relativism in which there is no truth and no grounds to prefer one moral position over another. It does not go with the fashionable ideology that exalts difference and abhors conceptualisation as the first falsehood. It recognises that we cannot have a world without moral diversity. But we can engage in the pursuit of what is humanly best. There is the possibility of learning from others, reaching perhaps a fusion of horizons. And the possibility of convincing others about the wisdom of one's own point of view. Indeed exposure to other moralities is part of inter-religious dialogue and may well contribute to a tradition's ongoing re-thinking of the more specifically religious dimension of its vision. If there is to be dialogue, what is most important is that each grouping is self-

---

13. See Jean Porter, *Natural and Divine Law: Redeeming the Tradition for Christian Ethics*, Grand Rapids, Erdmans, 1999, *passim*.

critical with an inner criticism, that it be in touch with its presuppositions, that it engage a hermeneutic of suspicion about its
well-worn traditions, that it be aware of unwarranted demands
on others. Tentativeness about one's positions, a readiness to
embrace a both/and rather than an either/or perspective might
sometimes even save lives.

How much agreement there will be in the concrete is another
matter. We are accustomed to disagreement in moral matters for
reasons already well flagged by Aristotle and Aquinas. Secular,
so-called rational, moralists disagree among themselves. What
interests us here is disagreement that is traceable to religious difference. As we have seen, most of those who engage in the debate on comparative religious ethics find areas or strands or
forms of agreement and are concerned to work out just how and
why. That seems to me to be right. It is important, in the midst of
the academic debate, not to lose sight of the degree of actual
overlap among traditions, religious and secular. There is a
strong spine of concern for the human running through many of
the great religions, often indeed deepened and enhanced by
their religious outlook. For example, there is almost universal
reaction to experiences and situations of dehumanisation.
Catastrophe and distress call forth worldwide response. There is
some common sense of the *humanum*. So there are grounds for
conversation. Because in the end, it would appear that human
life has certain ineradicable and defining characteristics that are
commensurable from one cultural or religious context to another
– but analogously.

Obviously the commonalities will be greater where the
worldviews are closer. But even among very divergent worldviews – Bahai, Buddhism, Confucianism, Christianity, Hinduism,
Jainism, Judaism, Islam, Shintoism, Sikhism, Zoroastrianism –
Küng has convincingly pointed to aspirations that have resonances for all.[14] That is not inconsiderable. The kind of joint statement which several religions have found possible to make from
time to time, for example in Britain with regard to end of life issues, is an important witness also, even if it does remain at the
general. Such aspirations also have resonances for a secular
morality. But to say that is not to gloss over the fact that any state
faces growing problems about issues fundamental to its basic
raison d'etre, particularly issues of life and rights, and issues of

14. Küng, *Global Responsibility*, 63.

autonomy and freedom, on which religions have profound convictions.

Church, State, Society

My main concern here has been to take some note of the logic and implications of religious morality. I come back briefly to the starting point that sent me on that trail – the relations of church and state in this country in a changed environment. We know that the ever-present temptation for an institution, as for the individual, is one of control. To seek conditions in society which favour its own style of life. To insist on the rightness of one's own vision rather than on a more inclusive vision of what the good of all, the common good, requires. Ultimately then to fail to respect the otherness and the sincerity of the other and the deep plurality which that calls for.

In fact religions take quite different positions about influence on public policy. Some states, of course, are theocracies. But in the modern liberal democracy a religion such as Catholicism which takes an optimistic view of human realities, which centres its moral teaching on natural law with its notions of reasoned discourse, human well-being and common good, and which expects its adherents to exercise the virtues that contribute to such good, will anticipate a ready dialogue partner in the state. It will not shrink from comment on matters moral but such comment will be offered as a contribution to the search for the good of society. But it will equally recognise that the common good which it advocates requires also a sensitive listening to an increasing number of other viewpoints, each with its own peculiarly wrought moral system.

On the other hand, it is interesting and instructive to consider that there is a strong conviction among some Protestant churches that one influences society better by the authority of the faith-community's life, though even here there are nuances of position: there are more or less detached stances. For some of them, the great mistake of Christian ethics is to try to do business with, to try to show its congruence with and relevance for the theories of modern liberal democracy: that is seen as blurring the vision of a church in society, taking the edge off its critical thrust. Such churches will opt to convince instead by the inspiration of their teaching and particularly by their witness in the cause of human well-being. They hope for a contagion of admiration, a recognition of the authenticity of their style of life.

One would hope that our state would recognise that citizens who are religious adherents are entitled to work towards what they see as the betterment of society by persuasion and respectful argument. One would expect a creative engagement in which religious faiths are acknowledged as among the component communities of the state and as important partners in public debate. They may well have preserved much that is valuable in the search for the genuinely human. Crimes committed in the name of religion have already been adverted to and cannot be gainsaid. But Roman Catholicism, at its best, and in communion with other traditions, insists on the sacredness of the individual and the centrality of community. It is committed to solidarity and justice. It is positive about life and the care of the cosmos. It can be a counterweight to cynicism, individualism and frivolous consumerism. It supports and offers powerful motivation for the whole moral enterprise. It holds out in its founder, like other great religions, a striking example of concern for society. It would be a tragedy if the accumulated wisdom of religious morality, however diverse, were not heard in the public square.

CHAPTER EIGHT

A discourse on the centrality of justice in moral theology

Enda McDonagh

In a new biblical fantasy world the Freedomites would be at perpetual war with the Justiceites while the Shalomites (Peaceniks) would be completely marginalised. And the Lords of the Western World would provide the arms. Perhaps not that much of a fantasy, as war is waged by the powerful in the name of freedom, without any real reference to justice or international law. Anyway justice usually means control by the major economic powers with at least the complicity of major and sometimes minor political powers. Globalisation from above, sometimes promoted or ensured by the military sky-gods, remains the dominant force in the modern world, while globalisation from below, from the powerless citizens of the world with all their theoretical equality in dignity, rights, freedom and justice, solidarity and peace, remain mere raw material in themselves or in what they supply for the current, self-appointed 'Masters of the Universe'.

In his theological and legal work, in service of students and prisoners, Patrick Hannon combined his theological insights, his legal and forensic skills and his elegant literary style to great effect. His earlier university studies in English literature and his years teaching English have made him one of the most readable writers of theology around. His doctoral studies in theology, on love and marriage in Augustine, provided him with capacity for critical and creative theological thought. His legal studies, leading to his being called to the Irish Bar, gave him the legal knowledge and precision which had been of such value to the Irish Episcopal Commission for Prisoners Overseas. More recently he has been writing clearly and effectively on issues of war and peace. In the 'real-fantasy' world of globalisation from the skies, with scant regard for the earth or its inhabitants, Patrick Hannon has much to offer to resisting peoples, resisting Christians and resisting theologians. In accordance with the wishes of the

Editor, this essay in his honour will concentrate on one of the focal points in his moral theology, justice. As practitioners of that discipline know only too well, it is impossible simply to separate justice from its 'natural' companions, freedom and peace, or from its Christian *fons et origo*, love / charity.

In moral discourse 'justice' is frequently regarded as the 'hard man' of the moral virtues. In religious discourse the justice of God may be used to terrify, with the God of the Hebrew scriptures in his punitive justice lazily contrasted with the God of Jesus Christ, the God of love who is Love. In Hebrew biblical terms the God of Israel is the God of creation, of promise / covenant and of forgiveness / reconciliation / renewal who is in a positive rather than punitive sense a God of justice and of loving-kindness, as their paralleling in the psalms among other historical, wisdom and prophetic writings affirms. All this is finally confirmed for New Testament readers and believers in Jesus' response to the query about which is the first commandment of the law, obviously the Mosaic Covenant Law. Loving God and your neighbour has its roots in that covenant but it becomes much more overt and central in the New Covenant established in the teaching, life, death and resurrection of the new Moses, Jesus Christ.

One way of illustrating this most effectively would be by comparing Moses' mountain charter, the Ten Commandments with Jesus' mountain charter, the Sermon on the Mount (in Matthew as against Luke, with his Sermon on the Plain). Some reflection on and dialogue between these two central moral manifestos may help in discerning the basics of biblical morality and indeed of biblical justice. A third partner in the dialogue would be that great, modern charter of Justice, the UN Declaration of Human Rights, 1948, with its antecedents and consequences.

The Ten Commandments were, as biblical scholars agree, the fruit of the interaction between different moral and religious traditions, and the existence of two different versions of the Sermon are found in the canonical gospels. Neither is it credibly claimed that either version represents as it stands the immediate composition of Jesus. The evangelists probably brought together from the oral traditions a series of connected insights and sayings attributable in various ways to Jesus, if not all utterly original. However, the Ten Words, as they are sometimes called, have a history after, as well as before, their being written down, and in the Christian church as well as in the later scriptures, commentaries and life of the People of the Mosaic Covenant, so that they are one of the truly formative moral influences in the wider Western world.

The manuals which dominated Catholic moral theology from the Council of Trent to the Second Vatican Council devoted one large volume to the Ten Commandments with justice treated, rather narrowly it must be admitted, under the seventh commandment, 'Thou shalt not steal'. As an alternative, particularly in manuals produced by the Dominicans, the virtues took precedence over the commandments in organisation, but in practical terms the virtue model moved very little beyond the treatment of justice under the rubric of the seventh commandment. However, of the Sermon on the Mount there was not a whisper in the manuals of either kind. That belonged not to the moral teaching of the church but to its counsels of perfection and 'spiritual' reading and direction, in so far as it figured at all outside the commentaries on the gospels in scripture studies. In fact the only New Testament reference in such moral theology was to Jesus' comments on divorce in the volume/section dealing with the sixth and ninth commandments. This was a separate volume for example in the Noldin-Schmidt manual, while marriage was treated in the volume on the sacraments and, as with the other sacraments, almost exclusively in canon law terms. Noldin-Schmidt remained a standard text-book well into the 1960s.

Moral Theology and the Medievals
In many scholars' estimation, including that of the distinguished moral theologian, Bernhard Häring, the introduction of private penance by the Irish monks in the seventh and eighth centuries, and their composition and circulation of (Irish) Penitentials, had a very negative, long-term effect on the development of moral theology. In that view moral theology was focused on sinful acts as matter for confession. This was also reflected in the *Summae Confessariorum* of the High Middle Ages which eventually issued in the post-Trent manuals, which were really textbooks for confessors to be used in the new, reformed training of priests. All this was compounded by the rapid development of canon law from the twelfth century on. Canon law influenced the development of moral theology in two important ways. Moral

obligations tended to be thought of more and more as legal obligations and more obligations of Christian living were in fact those of church or canon law. By the time of the manuals, in the volume on the sacraments, for example, most of the matter considered was church law. The treatment of justice in this context focused on acts of injustice between individuals such as stealing another's property without any attention to deeper personal issues such as the virtue of justice or broader social issues such as poverty and power.

A very different strand of 'moral theology' was developing at this time also, with the discovery of the Greek philosophers, particularly of Aristotle, and their influence on theologians. In terms of theological achievement at the time and of subsequent and continuing influence, St Thomas Aquinas was the key figure. It should be noted that he and his peers never used the term 'moral theology' and did not really have our distinctions of disciplines between scripture, dogmatic and moral theology. Theology was a single enterprise for them, embracing all the disciplines we now distinguish. Admittedly, Thomas did treat ethical or moral issues within the *Secunda Pars* of his *Summa*, with basic issues such as the *lex aeterna Dei* which included the *lex naturalis* and *lex nova* in the *Prima Pars* of the *Secunda Pars*. It should also be made clear that he sharply distinguished and separated *lex Dei* and its components from *lex humana* whether of church (*lex canonica*) or of state (*lex civilis*). Moral as distinct from legal issues came under the *lex Dei*. In another significant move, continuing his dialogue between Christianity and other traditions, as well as between Augustine and Aristotle, he distinguished the *lex nova* as founded in Christ and his revelation, which he described as inscribed in the heart of the Christian by the presence of the Holy Spirit.

It is this presence which integrates and transforms the moral virtues of the broader traditions, even the cardinal or hinge virtues as Aristotle and Aquinas call them, justice, courage, temperance and prudence, so that charity becomes the form of all the virtues. This is taken to mean that the activities proceeding from the moral virtues are for the Christian expressions of what Jesus called the first and second commandments, love of God and love of neighbour. In the further insight of John's gospel, they express God's self who is love, inscribed in our hearts, forming New Commandment, New Covenant, indeed in

Pauline terms New Creation. It is in this incarnational and re-
demptive context, with its transformative force, that the role of
justice in theological ethics or moral theology may be properly
understood and explicated, without undermining the central
secular and humanistic value of justice as frequently invoked
and applied in our Western world, if not always given adequate
analysis or foundation. The various past and current theories of
justice as affecting individual relations or entering into the
moral formation of society have much to contribute to moral
theology as well as to moral philosophy and to their value in enlightening the practice of justice. From Plato and Aristotle to
Augustine and Aquinas, from Luther and Calvin to Barth, from
Kant to Macintyre and Rawls, to select names almost at random,
complementary and conflicting strands of the Christian and
human theory/virtue/practice of justice have striven for recognition and integration. In this brief essay in theological ethics,
much of that must be taken for granted and some few strands
isolated in search for an exposition of justice as significant to the
discipline in which Patrick Hannon has so distinguished himself, contemporary Catholic moral theology.

Creation, Differentiation and Justice
The return to creation as a primary theological and indeed ethical resource for Christian theologians is overdue but developing
quite quickly. More disputable, but equally valuable, is the overcoming of the discontinuity between creation and redemption
and so between the God of the Old Testament or covenant and
the God of the New Testament or covenant, indeed in Paul's
phrase, of the new creation. And all this has important implications for justice in moral theology.

   In the Genesis and other biblical accounts the Creator God is
depicted as making and observing the universe as distinct from,
differentiated from Godself. 'God made the heavens and the
earth ... and saw that they were good.' In this vision of creation
both the differentiation, and so the difference or otherness of the
created world, is at once established and recognised/respected
as good, given its due in justice, as later moral terminology
might put it. Simultaneously, by these biblical accounts, the universe itself is progressively differentiated, from the division into
light and dark, ocean and dry land, through the different plants
and animals to the critical differentiation of humans from the

rest of the world ('And God saw that (they) were very good') and their differentiation as male and female individuals. At the level of human creation and differentiation, human justice in response to God (religion) and in response to one another becomes possible and mandatory as does human respect for the wider world in their stewardship of it. Aquinas picks up on this when he categorises religion as a subcategory of the cardinal virtue of justice. Contemporary writer George Steiner provides a striking Genesis-related image of human beings as 'Guests of Creation'. In all these visions and versions it is important to remember that creation is not a once for all completed divine action but a continuing activity of the Creator-God who remains engaged with humanity and the world as the Hebrew and Christian scriptures attest.

The justice of God in relation to creatures expresses the divine recognition of and commitment to their created worth and goodness as differentiated and in that sense set over against, other than God's self. Where human creatures fail to live up to this worth and goodness, and so fail to respond as they should, they are themselves guilty of injustice and incur the judgement of God. This judgement, which is frequently mentioned in both Old and New Testament, testifies to the reality of the differentiation, the freedom of humans and the authentic justice of God. Yet as noted above, it is a justice set within a richer divine reality. In the history of Israel, it is sometimes combined with that characteristic of God which in Hebrew is called *hesed*, meaning loving kindness as in Psalm 85 etc. The movement in the book by minor prophet Zephaniah from extended condemnatory judgement of all creation including Judah and Jerusalem by their God to merciful renewal is typical of so much of the whole Hebrew corpus. And the two great commands of the New Testament, love of God and love of neighbour, are already clearly proclaimed in the Old. In both Testaments, then, justice in the relationship between Creator and creatures is clearly demanded, yet contained within the overarching reality of love while lacking the equality which Aristotle thought crucial to strict justice. Justice between human beings themselves is an intrinsic component of both testaments and with serious attention to justice for the poor and marginalised. Indeed for Jeremiah to do justice is to know God, and for Amos neglect and exploitation of the weak renders worship of God futile. This attention to people on the margins is so characteristic of Jesus' ministry and teaching that it becomes the basis for final divine judgement in Matthew 24 for example. Yet it is justice and judgement in the context of the overriding power of the God who is love.

Guests of Creation
Before moving into some of the regular concerns of justice in moral theology which are normally confined to human relationships, both personal and social, it may be helpful to reflect a little further on the human condition as creature within a much larger creation as gift of the Creator-God. George Steiner's phrase does not necessarily include the recognition of such a divine Creator, although in such books as *Real Presences* and *Grammar of Creation*, he comes very close to it. However, I adopt the phrase to my own rather than his purposes, and without attributing such belief to him, I use it as expressing my own belief that as guests of creation we humans are also guests of the Creator. For a Christian theologian this is an obvious move, with important moral implications for our whole lives and for the moral reality of justice. As indicated above, equality on which many theories and practices of justice depend does not apply as between God and creatures, even human creatures. Yet the Jewish and Christian traditions emphasise the justice of God in dealing with human beings, but always tempered by loving mercy and forgiveness because of human limitations and failures. Mercy and forgiveness will also be seen to be a feature of just relationships between equals (i.e. humans) even if it has been neglected or ignored in much discussion of justice in moral theology and moral philosophy. The creaturehood of humans has other important implications which have often been distorted in theological circles by reducing human beings to blind obedience to divine commands as mediated by scripture, without due regard (in justice) for the proper processes of interpretation or the appropriate free response of human beings. As against the blind obedience error, the recognition of human creaturehood helps prevent the promethean reach to unlimited power by individuals or groups which is always at the expense of other individuals or groups and so unjust. History records many horrific instances of this overreaching in power and the consequent injustices, while today's news bulletins carry endless examples in destructive economic and political dominance.

A more subtle but no less destructive consequence of ignoring human creaturehood and our position as guests and not lords of creation, is human treatment of planet earth as simply humanity's own to dominate and exploit. There is a tradition of using Genesis 1:28 to justify human domination of the earth, often accompanied by accusations against Christianity of justifying the rape of the earth. That would certainly be an exaggeration. However, the overall biblical view of all animate and inanimate creation as reflecting God's glory and eliciting God's care offers a very different vision, of human beings as guests, admirers and stewards of creation who, at the same time as they cherish the earth, must with restraint live off it. Christianity then encourages an enjoyment of the earth's beauty, justice to its differentiated elements and a loving care for them by human beings set within the divine gift of creation. Too many even Christian defenders of ethics towards the environment rely too heavily on utilitarian arguments about the need to protect the earth's resources for the use of the present and future human generations without reflecting on and respecting its own beauty, mystery and integrity. Others reduce humans to being just one other species, removing the possibility of a true aesthetic and moral, let alone religious, response.

The final and perhaps most important challenge in this section is to differentiate the dignity and worth of human beings as essential to their equality by their all sharing in the divine dignity, without making them into godlings themselves, with all the power struggles and injustice that would involve towards one another and the environment, and without making morality and justice, including human rights, into some simply human, even arbitrary and perhaps disposable invention. For Jews and Christians, the rooting of human dignity in the divine gives each human being an equal and irreducible character as a secure basis for both their personal rights and responsibilities, including their responsibilities to the wider creation.

The Hard Core of Morality, Christian and Human
Encounters between Creator and creatures, between humans and their fellows, reveal the irreducible differences which exist between them, and the (moral) demand to recognise and respect these differences. To fail to do so, by ignoring or seeking to possess the other, is in the vision of Emmanuel Levinas to 'murder

them'. (We leave aside for the moment the encounters and relationships between humans and non-human creatures.) Levinas, like some modern philosophers/theologians, emphasises the human (and divine) other as the source and summons of morality. Without following him or others to the letter, it seems clear that moral call and response emerge in such encounters and are sustained in the continuing relationships within which people live, with one another and with their God. At the centre of such moral encounters and relationships is the summons to respect one another as persons in their irreducible differences, in their needs and gifts, in their rights and responsibilities. This is the hard core of morality, giving to one another our basic due of recognition and respect and responding to their particular need, exercising the virtue of justice to all.

From acceptance of this hard core of justice came the recognition of natural rights, later rights of man and now human rights, which play a key role in seeking to establish just societies and a just world. The United Nations' Declaration of Human Rights with its associated covenants and conventions, such as the European Convention, provide a basic platform for the promotion and protection of justice between and within countries. And despite gross violations of such rights, even in countries of their birth and development, they are an indispensable instrument of national and international politics and law in the pursuit of justice. Given the rigours of their formulation, their development in reach and application and their growing incorporation in law at national and international levels, human rights are one of humanity's great moral discoveries and achievements. In the Western tradition, from which in their modern form they emerged, they rank with the Jewish Decalogue and the Christian Sermon on the Mount as major shapers of our moral universe. Yet they do not and cannot stand alone. As many critics have observed, rights must always be balanced by accompanying responsibilities. While some of these critics may be defending their own or others' privileges, power and possessions against the deprived claiming their rights, an integral justice will combine regard for the responsibilities of all, with priority for the claims of those deprived of basic human rights and freedoms. The whole inhabited world bears witness to the difficulties of such combination. In Ireland we are still wrestling with such conflicting claims in Northern Ireland, with new conflicts over immigrants and asylum seekers and apparently the most intractable of all, those between the settled community and the traveller community.

A different form of criticism of the emphasis on human rights emerges from their perception and sometimes their exercise in purely individual terms. Despite the recognition of cultural, social and economic rights in the original charter and particular covenants, their Western provenance and dominant Western individualism have frequently restricted human rights to the political rights of individuals in society. Development of rights transcending the simply individual is in progress, although there is a long way to go. Apart from that, human rights cannot stand alone as the only bearers of morality between individuals and societies. Even the addition of responsibilities corresponding to each right would not provide an adequate framework for truly moral and human relationships and societies. Marriage, for example, must take seriously reciprocal rights and responsibilities but it needs more than that. So do so many other human relationships and institutions, moral values and practices. Without a basis in justice and so in rights and responsibilities, families and friendships, local communities and schools, churches and voluntary bodies from sporting organisations to justice seeking NGOs and political parties themselves could not survive. To thrive as human realities they need generosity and self-sacrifice, compromise, forgiveness and reconciliation and other moral practices which cannot be neatly pigeon-holed under rights, with or without the add-on of responsibilities. Justice itself is a larger word than rights, even in the current secular language of morality. In the Jewish and Christian traditions as we have seen it connects easily with loving-kindness and mercy on God's side and with religion and worship on the human side.

Justice and Forgiveness
As the hard core of morality, justice implies a strictness that might easily slip into unnecessary harshness. More dangerously it might be pursued in a vengeful manner that precludes the possibility of restoring the human relations, whose violation was clearly an offence against justice, between individuals or within society or both. The pursuit of justice through the courts, the compensation for the injury caused and, if necessary for the safety of society and the rehabilitation of the offender, the im-

prisonment of the convicted is not, in purely human terms, the end of the affair. The full human resolution lies in the restoration of relations between offended and offender and between offender and society. This involves for the injured party the completion of justice, the rendering of his due to the other, in the traditional definition, by forgiveness which can only result in reconciliation, the restoration of true human relationships by the return, repentance, conversion of the offending other. If this is rare in the practice of criminal or other forms of justice, it may be because it is ignored in moral, civic and legal education. In theological education there is no excuse for its omission. At the practical level of the sacrament of penance, forgiveness and restoration of relationship with God and community are central. In the biblical understanding of justice, as we have seen, it is closely related to mercy and so to forgiveness. The dynamic justice of God as expressed in continuing divine creation has forgiveness at its leading edge, as God seeks to renew or restore right(eous) relationships with creatures. As Christians we pray each day as taught by Jesus, 'Our father … forgive us our trespasses as we forgive those who trespass against us.' Jesus, forgiving his enemies on the cross, remains our teacher and model. For the just man who falls seven times every day, forgiving seventy times seven seems hardly excessive. And we have in personal experience or in the media our regular human models amidst the domestic and political conflicts which afflict us. For Irish consolation and inspiration Gordon Wilson's forgiveness of the killers of his daughter who died as he held her hand was deeply significant. Only by combing justice with such forgiveness will reconciliation and peace be restored as Mohandas Gandhi, Martin Luther King, Nelson Mandela and so many others knew so well.

Freedom, Justice and Peace

In developing and teaching moral theology, a series of difficult dialogues between theory and practice, between sacred and secular traditions, and many others is required. One of the more useful dialogues for addressing social issues may be between the Jewish-Christian vision of freedom, justice and peace and the modern triad of liberty, equality and fraternity. As I have attempted this at some length elsewhere, (*The Gracing of Society*, Dublin, 1990), I will concentrate on the biblical vision and its development here while keeping the terms associated particularly with the French Revolution in the background. In the order presented here, justice is placed between freedom and peace and not by accident but by theology. The freedom of the Creator was primary and was shared with human creatures from their beginning. The differentiation between Creator and creatures involved the recognition and respect for difference and its demands which is called justice, divine justice and human justice. Such justice could only be freely and fully exercised in community, in reconciling relationships, in peace. The kiss of justice and peace as envisioned in Psalm 85 may be never more than partially realised in history, but it is the goal towards which all human beings are called to strive after. The blessed justice-seekers and blessed peace-makers of the Sermon on the Mount must eventually freely include all humankind, believing and unbelieving alike. Of such is the kingdom of God for such is God. The ultimate divine mystery of the Triune God might be briefly if crudely invoked here in its distinctive persons as the freely creating Father, the justifying Son and the bonding and peace-making Spirit. At least the moral theologian may never evade that unifying and differentiating mystery, however deeply s/he must enter into the tangled undergrowth of human relations, rights and responsibilities.

Globalisation and the Reign of God
Of the moral dialogues referred to above, for theologians and above all moral theologians who focus on justice, the most important may be that between the current phenomena of globalisation and the present and eschatological realisation of the kingdom or reign of God. Once again I excuse myself from any extended discussion as I have already treated the subject at some length in the forthcoming publication on globalisation in the series *Christian Perspectives on Development* (Veritas/Trócaire/Cafod, Dublin, 2005). However, the connection between these two great symbols, of the secular and sacred respectively, and their realisation, partially and ambiguously in both cases I believe, puts great strain on the moral practices and theories of justice. For too many people, religious or no, globalising, as I prefer to call it, is purely a matter of economics and technology. Add in the dominant ideology of the free market and globalising readily becomes economic colonialism, even imperialism. The threatened reduction of all the peoples and cultures of the world

to economic units and processes at the bidding of powerful corporations and states is too awful to contemplate and will in any
case meet with stiff resistance. The struggle for economic justice
is worldwide and is gradually intensifying. Guidelines for such
a justice will depend on the vision and will of many partners, including grassroots victims of the present process as well as
NGOs, trade unions, corporations who are not simply driven by
greed and can also see how self-interest may be served by more
just arrangements for trade and aid in what must eventually become much more of a globalising from the bottom up. At the
same time, due respect must be accorded to different cultural
and religious traditions where they do not obviously offend
justice themselves. All this requires economic, political, cultural
and religious dialogue of a kind that will promote a more free,
just and peaceful world, thus realising something of the
Christian vision of the reign of God.

CHAPTER NINE

Moral discourse in a time of AIDS

Suzanne Mulligan

It is probably fair to say that within Catholic moral theology discussion of the AIDS pandemic has been largely confined to the area of sexual morality. Debates about the use of condoms as prophylactics tend to dominate ethical discourse on this matter. The magisterium insists on the Christian ideals of abstinence before marriage and fidelity to one's spouse within marriage, not only as the safest way of avoiding infection, but also as the morally correct way of combating the current crisis. Although there are notable exceptions to this rather sweeping statement, it remains the case that the sexual ethics dimension of the problematic gains greatest attention within moral theology, and even then questions concerning the use of condoms achieve considerable (some would say excessive) time and discussion.

It is unfortunate that ethical discourse about AIDS is so closely associated with debates about condoms, not because this is an unimportant question but because it has resulted in other aspects of the problematic being overlooked or ignored. The complexities of the global AIDS pandemic reach far beyond theological discussions about condom use. Moral theologians are beginning to redress the imbalance by focusing on matters pertaining to justice and human rights, and their relevance to the spread of HIV/AIDS. It may perhaps be helpful to briefly examine some of the central moral arguments arising from discourse about condoms before moving to some of the more fundamental aspects of this issue. In 'AIDS – Some Theological and Moral Issues'[1] Patrick Hannon observes that:

> Underlying these arguments [about condom use where someone is HIV positive] are important questions of theory which have been the subject of debate among moral theologians during the past two decades or so: questions about objectivity in moral judgement, the universality of moral

---

1. Patrick Hannon, 'AIDS – Some Theological and Moral Issues', *The Furrow*, Vol 42, No 2 (February 1991), 71-79.

norms, the claims of personal conscience *vis-à-vis* the teaching of the magisterium of the Catholic Church. This debate was stimulated by the publication of *Humanae Vitae*, though it is both more fundamental and more far-reaching than are the specific concerns of that encyclical. It is not likely to be over any more quickly than the debate on the teaching of *Humanae Vitae*.[2]

Fifteen years on and arguments about those same questions still abound. *Humanae Vitae* condemned all acts of deliberate artificial contraception, labelling them 'intrinsically wrong'. In the context of HIV/AIDS, many theologians have explored the possibility of using condoms as one means of reducing transmission rates. The Doctrine of Double Effect, the Doctrine of Cooperation, and the Principle of the Lesser Evil have been invoked in the hope that they might resolve the dilemma. Some argue that in the context of AIDS condoms are being used as prophylactics not as contraception, and thereby do not contradict the teaching of *Humanae Vitae*.[3]

Despite this, and the amount of time diverted to the question of condom use, it appears as though the issue of condoms and AIDS is no nearer resolution. Yet, as one comes to understand more about this particular pandemic, one realises that the question of condoms is peripheral at best. More basic questions concerning justice and human rights need to be addressed before one can speak meaningfully about the sexual ideals promoted by the Catholic magisterium.

Therefore, some of these more fundamental concerns will be examined here rather than re-opening the debate about condoms. Although concentration will rest mainly on the situation in the developing world, the issues examined ought to be the concern of all. Within Ireland we see that many of these areas are receiving attention from the government in its oversees development aid, as well as being the focus of many Irish NGOs.

---

2. Ibid., 75.
3. See, for example, John Tuohey, 'Methodology or Ideology: The Condom and a Consistent Sexual Ethic', *Louvain Studies*, Vol 15, (1990), 52-69. Also, Jon D. Fuller and James F. Keenan provide an overview of this debate in 'Church Politics and HIV Prevention: Why is the Condom Question So Significant and So Neuralgic?', Linda Hogan, Barbara FitzGerald (eds), *Between Poetry and Politics*, Dublin, Columba Press, 2003, 158-181.

   As mentioned above, the AIDS pandemic raises many moral questions other than those pertaining to the licitness or otherwise of condom use. An understanding of the complexities of the crisis, and an adequate theological response, requires inclusion, therefore, of the many other dimensions of the pandemic. Hannon observes that 'When Christian teachers speak on the moral issues raised by AIDS they are at least equally bound to address the broader moral canvas as they are to deal with the relevant sexual ethic.'[4] This broader moral canvas includes the justice dimension of the problematic. Hannon also makes a point that is only beginning to be fully realised within Catholic moral theology.

> [T]he blame for failure to live up to what Christians consider the ideal in sexual relationships or in relationships generally is sometimes more properly to be laid at the door of our societies; that there are features of our world – including our Irish world – which make life intolerable for certain kinds of people, so that they are driven to drugs or to a futile search for comfort in the kind of casual sex which puts them at risk of the AIDS virus. It is a sombre reminder that a comfortable obliviousness to such realities makes us, even if remotely, co-contributors to the spread of the disease.[5]

Hannon's words are perhaps best understood in relation to the epidemic within the developing world. During the 1990s, as the full horror of AIDS emerged in Africa and South America, it became clear that there were in fact 'features of our world', manmade features in many cases, which pushed both individuals and entire communities into a situation where this disease would flourish. The context within which transmission generally occurs in these countries demonstrates how poverty and deprivation often force people into high-risk activity as a means of survival, at least in the short term.

Poverty and AIDS
One of the key elements in the spread of HIV/AIDS within the developing world is poverty, in its various guises. The connection between poverty and AIDS has been well documented. It is widely accepted that those who are poorest among us are at

4. Hannon, 'AIDS – Some Theological and Moral Issues', 73.
5. Ibid., 73.

greatest risk of infection. This is true within countries of the North also where we find that the poorer or more marginalised groups within society are more likely to engage in high-risk behaviour such as drug abuse and casual sexual liaisons, as a means of either survival or of short-term escape from the harshness of life. Nevertheless, the majority of people infected with this disease reside in the poorer countries of the South. An examination of the pandemic in the developing world illustrates this link between poverty and AIDS.

It is estimated that almost 70% of the total population infected with HIV/AIDS live in sub-Saharan Africa. Thirty million Africans are thought to be living with the disease. In some African countries HIV prevalence among adults now exceeds 30%; in Zimbabwe, Botswana, Namibia, Lesotho, and Swaziland at least 30% of the adult population are HIV positive.[6] For many years, South Africa had been labelled the 'AIDS capital of the world'. India has since been crowned with that unenviable title, and estimates suggest that there are already 5.6 million people living with the disease in India alone.

It is no coincidence that the majority of those infected with HIV/AIDS live in the third world, for poverty drives people into situations that greatly increase the likelihood of infection. So-called 'survival strategies' such as prostitution often result in exposure to the AIDS virus. Many living in poverty are unable to avoid the type of activity which can place them at risk of contracting HIV. In circumstances of severe poverty, women and young girls are forced to exchange sex for food or money; their bodies are their only marketable commodity and their best hope of providing for their families. Indeed, we find that in Burma and other parts of the Far East, parents are hoping to have female children since these girls will later become a source of income for the family, usually by being sold into the sex industry. For many, meeting short-term survival needs generally takes priority over protecting one's long-term health needs.

The impoverished condition of many third world countries is largely, although by no means exclusively, a creation of the developed nations of the North. Unequal trade agreements between North and South, unjust lending terms for international loans, and crippling third world debt is all but eliminating poorer

6. See for example Enda McDonagh, Ann Smith, *The Reality of HIV/AIDS*, (Trócaire, Veritas, CAFOD, 2003), 20.

nations' ability to achieve strong economies. The resulting lack of financial resources for health care services, education, and job creation inevitably hits those who are already vulnerable within society the hardest. Poor nutrition, unemployment, lack of medical and social facilities, leaves few options for millions who are trying to survive.

Although poverty facilitates the transmission of HIV/AIDS, it is also true to say that AIDS in turn increases poverty. It is no surprise that where a large percentage of the working populations (fifteen to forty nine years) are infected with HIV the economy suffers. Development strategies are failing, and economic targets simply cannot be achieved since those considered most productive within society ('productive' from an economic/financial perspective) are sick or dying.

In addition, because it is very often the breadwinner of the family who becomes infected, individual families suffer financially.[7] Extra medical expenses, special dietary requirements, loss of income, and funeral costs, leave already struggling families in a precarious situation. Where both parents die from AIDS, older children are generally left with the responsibility of caring and providing for other siblings. Girls may feel that sex is their only means of providing food and shelter for younger siblings. Thus, the AIDS-poverty cycle is extremely difficult to break. As Christians, we are called to solidarity with those members of the Body of Christ who are suffering and dying. Our moral responsibility is even greater when we consider that much of the poverty is, in part at least, our collective creation.

Gender and AIDS
The contribution of gender inequality to the global spread of AIDS is another factor that needs examination. Here too one sees how the AIDS pandemic raises questions pertaining to justice and human rights. Within many societies women are not afforded the same rights as men. Inequality within relationships and lack of social, political, and economic empowerment place women at particular risk of infection. Gender affects men too, and one

---

7. Clearly the emotional trauma of losing a loved one to AIDS is beyond calculation. I do not wish to suggest that the loss to any family ought only to be seen in a monetary way, but the aim here is to point to the added financial burdens of AIDS for individual families as well as for countries as a whole.

finds that expectations to live up to male 'ideals' can often lead to engagement in high-risk sexual behaviour. In certain parts of Cape Town, for example, young men are reported to boast about their HIV status, since to be HIV positive implies that one is sexually experienced.

Women's economic dependency on their husbands or male relatives can leave them with little control over their sexual lives. It is ironic that for many women marriage poses the greatest risk of becoming infected. A woman's inferior status within society and within the marital relationship itself means that she is unable to negotiate the use of condoms should she suspect her husband of infidelity. Thus, for many women the question of whether or not condom use is moral/immoral is irrelevant to their situation.

Noting the effect that the social and economic subordination of women has on transmission rates, Kevin Kelly explains that preventative work based solely on change in sexual behaviour is bound to fail. Rather, change must occur at the social level as well.[8] Kelly describes the 'double-standard morality' often evident within sexual relationships, and concludes:

> In the light of the picture presented above, it would seem unrealistic and even harmful to suggest that the only real solution to the HIV/AIDS pandemic lies in the traditional 'faithful to one partner' sexual ethic. That offers no help to many women. For them, what is lacking is the very foundation without which such a sexual ethic is virtually meaningless. As long as their full and equal dignity is not accepted in theory and in practice, many of the norms of this traditional sexual ethic are likely to work against the well-being of these women and may even prove to be the occasion of their becoming infected by HIV.[9]

Indeed Kelly suggests that the Catholic church's teaching on sexual ethics may in fact be part of the problem rather than part of the solution. It therefore seems that any response to the AIDS pandemic which places an exclusive focus on sexual promiscuity, on condoms, or other related issues, fails to appreciate the fact that sexual behaviour is strongly influenced by the economic and social conditions of one's life. Consequently, a decision to

8. Kevin Kelly, *New Directions in Sexual Ethics: Moral Theology and the Challenge of AIDS*, (London: Geoffrey Chapman, 1998), 3.
9. Ibid., p 8ff.

live by the sexual ideals promoted by the Catholic Church is only possible where one's social circumstances allow for the realisation of such ideals. The role of freedom here is critical; understanding how social, political and economic circumstances diminish, or even take away completely, one's freedom to choose a certain way of life is vital.

One major obstacle for those trying to contain the spread of HIV/AIDS is the current level of rape and sexual violence experienced by many women. Apart from the obvious difficulties this poses for containing HIV/AIDS, sexual violence also violates women's basic rights.[10] The long-term task of securing equal rights and justice for women ought to be at the core of proposed solutions to the pandemic. Obviously solutions based on change in attitude towards women is a long-term goal, and something which will not be achieved immediately. However, since evidence demonstrates how the spread of HIV through heterosexual activity is greatly aided by the inferiority of women, it is important to focus attention on promoting and protecting women's rights and dignity. Long-term preventative efforts must target this aspect of the pandemic.

Disturbingly, the number of sexual attacks on young children is becoming more common in certain countries also. In South Africa, for example, attacks of this nature are on the increase. Infants as young as four months old have been targeted. These assaults are largely fuelled by sexual myths suggesting that intercourse with a virgin or young child will cure a person of AIDS. Obviously such myths place children and infants at enormous risk of infection.

Therefore, moral responses to the epidemic in the third world that are based solely on traditional sexual ethics offer little hope to millions of people living in poverty or living in abusive and unequal sexual relationships. It is not the intention here to trivialise or dismiss the importance of much of the Catholic Church's sexual teaching or the values contained within it.[11] But it is argued that the social and economic conditions affecting people's sexual activity must also be carefully analysed and incorporated into magisterial responses to the pandemic.

---

10. It is not the author's intention to imply that women are the only group who suffers sexual violence. In some countries such as South Africa male rape is a major problem within prisons. Here, however, I wish to concentrate on sexual violence directed at women.

Access to Medication

The importance of the human rights aspect of AIDS cannot be emphasised enough. Some have argued for the 'human right to health',[12] in the sense that all human beings ought to have the right to basic food, shelter and medical supplies which contribute to a health and wellbeing. However, unless financial resources are made available for education and health care facilities – services essential to combating AIDS – long-term responses to the pandemic will remain inadequate.

There has been much public debate in recent times about the provision of cheaper antiretroviral (ARV) drugs for those living in poorer nations. The problem is not just that these drugs are so expensive, and therefore exclude millions from the possibility of ever benefiting from them. Nor is it simply that governments cannot afford to supply essential medication to their people.

One feature of antiretroviral therapies is that these drug regimes demand constant adherence, which in turn requires close supervision by trained nurses and healthcare workers in order to ensure responsible and correct consumption. This presupposes that a country has the necessary social and medical infrastructure to provide such supervision. Clinics, hospitals, specially trained doctors and nurses, as well as the appropriate equipment and medical supplies, are essential. Yet poverty and re-allocation of scarce funds for debt repayment means that many countries are unable to provide these facilities.

In addition, there are usually strict dietary conditions attached to the consumption of ARVs. The therapies are often complex and difficult, although newer drugs are less demanding in this regard. In some cases ARV regimes may involve tak-

---

11. Indeed in some countries we have seen the positive results of promoting abstinence and fidelity as ways of avoiding HIV infection. In Uganda, for example, there has been a decline in infection rates in recent years mainly because this approach was adopted by the Ugandan Government and by the major religious groups. But Uganda's success rests on other factors also, and it is not clear that the positive results experienced in Uganda could be replicated everywhere else, at least in the immediate future.

12. See for example Tony Evans, 'A Human Right to Health?', *Third World Quarterly*, Vol 23, No 2, (2002), 197-215. Paul Hunt makes a similar argument in 'The Right to Health: from the Margins to the Mainstream', *The Lancet*, Vol 360, (December 7, 2002), 1878.

ing up to thirty tablets daily.[13] Some tablets may need to be taken with water, others with food, some need to be taken a certain length of time before or after food, and they need to be taken at the same time each day. In countries where food shortages exist, and where people are undernourished and may live on a single meal a day (or less), such rigid requirements are impossible to meet. Also, side-effects can be severe and debilitating. Fatigue, vomiting, and nausea can result in a patient forgetting to take a dose. An under-funded and ill-equipped health service cannot adequately monitor patients and offer them the support and care that is needed.

In an attempt to obtain money or food, some people sell their medication illegally to others. Lack of information can lead people to think that a single dose of ARVs will cure them of AIDS. The hopelessness of poverty makes the black market sale of medication too attractive to resist. However, even a short break in a treatment regime of ARVs can lead to resistance to that medication. Should the virus subsequently be passed on to another person it will be a resistant form that is transmitted for which the original medication will be useless.

Thus, it is vital not only that individuals have access to antiretroviral drugs and other AIDS medication, but also that clear and accurate information is provided about the responsibilities of these drugs. Medical and social structures need to be in place to meet the demands of AIDS illnesses. However, this requires money and investment. Impoverished communities are often unable to meet the basic health needs of their people. The difficulties associated with AIDS medication mentioned here ought not be used as justification for the failure to provide people with ARVs, but rather as an incentive to ensure that all have adequate health care services and have access to basic medication.

Conclusion

It is hoped that the above account sufficiently illustrates that the underlying causes of apparent 'irresponsible' sexual behaviour are often linked to unjust social and economic pressures that are beyond the control of many people. The international community, for the most part, is slow to respond to the gravity of this situ-

---

13. Drugs are now been developed that are less demanding and are easier to take. But they are unlikely to be available to people in the Developing World in the near future.

ation. Within the theological community there is a responsibility to discuss these and other injustices associated with the spread of AIDS. Debates about condoms, and solutions based on fidelity go so far. They are certainly an important part of the debate but one must question their dominance within moral discourse on AIDS.

Within Catholic theology one finds a wealth of teaching on human rights, justice, human dignity, and various social and economic concerns, which could provide a more holistic approach to understanding the AIDS pandemic. Although there is no simple or single solution to the prevention and containment of AIDS, is it possible that the social teaching of the church could offer a great deal to the way we think about this problem. Catholic social teaching could provide a framework of analysis which would emphasise the mutual rights and responsibilities of all, and thereby allow for broader and more inclusive discussion of the pandemic. The social, cultural, political and economic factors in the spread of HIV would be seriously debated, in turn allowing for greater dialogue with non-religious groups involved in preventative work.

Catholic sexual ethics, and especially the moral questions raised by the use of condoms as prophylactics, has dominated moral discourse on AIDS in the past. A redressing of this imbalance must be achieved in order for Christian theology to respond effectively to the needs and suffering of those living with this disease. And as Patrick Hannon reminds us, 'The Christian vision is above all a stimulus to Christians to take their place, courageously and with humility, alongside all who work for justice in the world'.[14]

14. Hannon, 'Rights: Theological Resources', *Milltown Studies*, Vol 42 (1998), 112.

CHAPTER TEN

A discourse on where ethical principles meet Christian experience

Denis O'Callaghan

Looking back over close on fifty years as a priest, the trajectory of life for me divides roughly half and half between teaching moral theology in Maynooth and serving as parish priest in Mallow. At the midway mark in that earlier period came the Second Vatican Council.

It has been a roller-coaster of a journey where milestones flashed by at a rate of knots. I now welcome the opportunity to review the process of analysing ethical principles on the back of Christian experience. In this I am somewhat like the Japanese tourist who typically keeps the camera glued to his eye when abroad and once he gets home he has time to find out where he has been! The review process will be a kind of theological/pastoral Odyssey.

Like all clerical students of the time I was introduced to textbook theology. It was a tight comprehensive system. We looked on our professors of theology as nigh omniscient. As an Oxford wit wrote of an arrogant professor: 'I am the master of the college. What I do not know is not knowledge.' We in Maynooth were not singular in this. The approach would have been common case in the other Irish universities of the time.

I am really grateful to one of my teachers in Maynooth for pointing me in a direction off the beaten path when I undertook postgraduate work. Fr John Hackett, Professor of Greek, was of a shy self-deprecatory nature when it came to displaying scholarship, which often ranged well beyond his formal subject matter. Just back in The Dunboyne House of Postgraduate Studies I met him at the door. It proved providential in the event. He mentioned a Benedictine, a Dom Odo Casel, who had died within the previous ten years. He suggested that, with some familiarity with Greek philosophy and literature, Casel's concept of sacrament might serve as a subject for research. The Paschal Mystery was at the heart of his theology. Dom Odo's particular insight was to link the concepts of Greek philosophy and mystery-religion with the development of the Christian theology of sacrament. He pointed out that the most influential early theologians were Greek in mind. They represented a providential *vorschule* of how the church came to express its faith. I well recall how Dr Gerard Mitchell, Professor of Dogmatic Theology, expressed his doubts about the viability of the theme. He said that a dissertation should be a vehicle to cross the river to the other bank, not to launch out on a current to God knows where! Anyway John Hackett offered to start me on the road, a road which would later reveal Dom Odo Casel as one of the architects of the theology of liturgy in the Constitution *Sacrosanctum Concilium* of the Second Vatican Council. It was a first experience for me of how visionary theology could become in the hands of a prophetic thinker. It certainly taught the lesson that there were different ways of approaching and analysing theological concepts other than the scholastic approach. In his Regensburg lecture on faith and reason in 2006, Pope Benedict XVI showed how important Greek philosophical concepts were to Christian reflection.

In our seminary training there was one factor which set the trend and coloured the overall theological culture. This was the Code of Canon Law promulgated in 1918. It had been compiled under the direction of Cardinal Pietro Gasparri, a gifted scholar and a superb canonist in his own right. One appreciates the extent and quality of the work from the myriad fonts or sources which had to be sifted through and collated. Imagine if today a group of legal scholars had undertaken the task of digesting and collating the decisions and precedents of the Common Law of England along with the subsequent statutory instruments into a single legal system parallel to France's *Code Napoleon*! Later on, when I came to complete postgraduate studies in Canon Law in Rome, the work that had gone to produce the 1918 Code left me in awe.

It was understandable how the finished product, described by one canonist, the late Cardinal William Conway, as having the structure and balance of a Roman arch, came to have an influence outside its particular domain in the study programme of the seminary. The Code provided a template in particular for the choice of method in moral theology. Indeed, our professors in moral theology had also doctorate degrees in Canon Law. The two disciplines ran in tandem. The only dissenting voice from the unquestioning worship of the Code was Fr Edmund O'Brien, qualified as a pre-Code canonist, then parish priest of Clondalkin in Dublin. He taught a course in the Maynooth Faculty of Canon Law. His concern was that the flexibility and room for pastoral discretion which had operated within the range of the fonts in pre-Code canon law had been sacrificed on the altar of the Code.

Coincidentally, when I came to study canon law in Rome in the early sixties I appreciated what Ned O'Brien was about. My particular area of study was on the principle in canon 21 of the 1918 Code. This established that a law made to meet a general or common danger extended its obligation to individuals in whose cases the particular danger was not verified. Intriguingly, Gasparri did not cite any fonts for that principle in canon 21. In earlier times this law had been described as a law based on a presumption. On research it emerged that the presumption in those cases in support of freedom from the obligation of general law had been removed, not by decision of church authority, but by consensus between three leading Jesuit canonists around 1600, Suarez, Vasquez and De Salas. Whether or not they were correct in their assessment need not concern us here, even though the principle is still very relevant on such practical issues as driving with a measure of alcohol over the legal limit. What the background research revealed was the broad field in which moral discernment and equity had operated in earlier times. As time went on, law became more absolute. The Code of Canon Law was the predictable result.

The sojourn in Rome gave space for attending moral theology conferences particularly in the Gregorian and Alphonsianum Universities. The overall approach of Josef Fuchs and Bernhard Häring was a revelation. They were free spirits, very learned and deeply spiritual. It was a liberating experience which opened heart and mind as the Second Vatican Council dawned. 'Bliss it was in that dawn to be alive. To be young was very heaven.'

As the Council was in preparation Rome became a hothouse of debate. One exciting side show was the confrontation between the Biblicum and the Lateran University on the principles of biblical hermeneutic. The launch of the campaign would seem to have been a pre-emptive strike. It was anticipated that the place of scripture would be crucial in setting out the direction of

Christian faith and life in what was to be a pastoral Council. The general intent of the reactionaries was to rule out of court these latter day 'modernists' in the field of biblical hermeneutic. The contest was medieval in its emotional charge, a virtual battle of Titans and Centaurs as bands of students from both schools of thought handed out fliers and pamphlets to the public.

The Lateran group commissioned spokespersons with strong backroom support in Rome for the traditional conservative line promoted by the Biblical Commission. The Biblicum drafted in an international array of scholars from the Ecole Biblique in Jerusalem and from various centres of learning in Europe and the United States. That combined firepower was awesome. It was not a contest between equals. It was reported at the time that Pope John XXIII had intervened behind the scenes to quell the continuing debate, reading its spirit as a disservice to the church. It would have mirrored the action of Clement VIII in 1594 in moving to calm the confrontation between Thomists and Molinists on questions of grace and free will. All this was exciting stuff in Rome at the time even though it received little coverage in the Irish media. Unfortunately my file on the debate, which included most of those fliers and pamphlets, has been lost. The debate also brought lasting regret that one did not have the opportunity to immerse oneself in the study of scripture with so much scholarship on offer. It was evident that the seminary tradition of moral theology suffered lack of direction here.

Meanwhile a number of us interested in moral theology would have been attending conferences at the various universities. I was particularly attracted to Bernhard Häring in the Alphonsianum. As a Redemptorist he was an admirer of St Alphonsus Liguori, the founder of the Order. St Alphonsus had been rightly famed for his pastoral sense in meeting people at where they were and in leading them to the challenge of moral truth. Alphonsus had taken a stand against rigorism or tutiorism in the application of moral norms. He had accepted the line of probabilism which allowed for discretion in choice of moral judgement where there were differing views on the force of the law. It amazed me that Bernhard Häring knew of a certain 'Padre Dinneen' who had written on probabilism. The said author had been a priest of my home diocese of Cloyne. He had been awarded the first doctorate in the Faculty of Theology at Maynooth after the college had been established as a Pontifical

University in 1895. It is likely that Häring would have heard about him from Fr Sean O'Riordan, a Redemptorist colleague on the staff at the Alphonsianum.

In his conferences, Häring followed a form of Socratic method. Probing and asking right questions featured more than arriving at final answers. His basic ideas would later be formulated in his monumental three volume work *The Law of Christ*. His scheme of moral theology was focused on two closely related factors – sacred scripture as the inspiration for Christian life and grace-instilled virtue as motivation for Christian behaviour. This placed moral theology in a different light to that of our textbooks. Once you accepted dependence on those two related fulcra that theology became pastoral of its very nature.

Formerly study of scripture for me had been the analysis and literal exegesis of the text. A useful exercise without question but the spiritual message had not engaged heart and mind as it did with Häring. Similarly with his bringing forward the approach of St Thomas in presenting moral behaviour as reflecting the internal force of virtue rather than the external observance of norms. Conscience flowed from internal conviction, from having one's heart in the right place, as Jesus taught in the Sermon on the Mount. Häring constantly referred to the French tradition of moral theology, which he saw as supremely pastoral as against the more academic analytic approach of his German counterparts. That French tradition went on to become the major influence on the Vatican Council. It certainly had the support of Pope John XXIII.

Another theme close to the heart of Häring was the concept of an Existential Ethic, which had been recently brought into focus by Karl Rahner. He saw that the outlawing of Situation Ethics had led to an overkill on the more positive personal side of Christian ethic. The resultant stress by church authority on the binding force of objective universal norms left the imperative of the individual vocation out of the equation.

This Existential Ethic can amount to a concrete moral demand on the individual in his particular circumstance. Christian morality should not then be presented simply as a morality of general rules and ecclesiastical directives. Christian conscience is called on to discern the will of God over and above these in terms of the talents, graces and opportunities which are placed in one's way. To quote Rahner himself: 'Norms are universal, but man as an existent is individual and unique in each case, and hence he cannot be regulated in his actions only by material norms of a universal kind.' This brings into play how St Thomas Aquinas defined the virtue of prudence as positive decision-making rather than just pastoral caution.

It is evident that here we have a clear reflection of what Jesus taught in the gospel. The Parable of the Talents is a good model of the Existential Ethic. 'To whom more is granted from him more is expected.' In other words the individual *will* be called to meet the universal norm in his or her particular way and *may* be called on to go beyond what it generally requires. Look at Zacchaeus shinning down that sycamore tree committing himself to paying over the odds in restitution!

It is not a comfortable ethic. One cannot take pride in judging oneself better than others. We simple do not know the limitations which they experience. 'We are unprofitable servants. We have done no more than what we were supposed to do.'

Then, of course, there was Häring the man and the priest. Naturally he had our respect for the courageous manner in which he had led home a group of German soldiers marooned on the Russian front after the defeat at Stalingrad. He was a priest of convinced vocation and profound spirituality as was evident in his public conferences and private conversations. He had been invited on one occasion at least to conduct the annual Vatican retreat. He lived in a spartan environment with most of the space in his small room taken up by a pallet bed and a desk surrounded with books. On my last visit to him, he was at his desk as usual barely able to converse because of a cancer of the throat which was to prove terminal.

I returned to Maynooth just as the council was about to begin. I returned with great expectations but it was a matter of *festina lente*. Fr John O'Flynn, Professor of Scripture, recommended that where seminarians were concerned one should not open a door which one might not be able to close. He followed his own advice. He kept to the beaten track in his teaching. Yet, as we found after his death, his personal line of study featured contemporary authors about whom he had not spoken to us. What a pity that was! His reservation would have been a relic of the sanctions on Modernism which in a former generation had restricted scholarly freedom in the study of scripture. That same censorious policy was soon to affect moral theology and keep moralists in a strait jacket.

Meanwhile the Second Vatican Council was moving ahead. In paragraph 16 of its 1965 Decree On the Training of Priests (*Optatam Totius*)*it* called for special attention to be given to the development of moral theology, which should be inspired by training in scripture and should present the challenge of the Christian vocation. A few months later the council promulgated the far-reaching Constitution On the Church in Today's World (*Gaudium et Spes*). This certainly marked out lines for a pastoral moral theology across a broad horizon.

At the time, in the pastoral approach to teaching moral theology, I was making much use of that dual witness observed in Christ's pastoral ministry, the witness to truth and the witness to compassion. That is seen in operation in the story of the woman taken in adultery. Jesus shows understanding of her plight but he does direct that she avoid sinning in future. The witness to compassion is well expressed in the Greek term *synkatabasis*, literally condescension, a process of coming to understand where people are at. Without it the witness to truth is coldly authoritarian. In turn, without that challenge of truth the appeal to compassion will descend into permissiveness and moral anarchy.

The value of that pastoral approach was soon to be tested in the controversy that followed *Humanae Vitae*. The encyclical was immediately raised to the status of touchstone, determining orthodoxy right across the moral spectrum. The issue turned on literal assent/dissent to the norm rather than on pastoral assessment of the human predicament. Episcopal conferences across the world issued directions on the application of the principles. Moral law and conscience, objective and subjective morality, became familiar terms of reference. Looking back over the spectrum of responses, the statement from the bishops of France would seem to have found the right pastoral balance. Häring's assessment of that French tradition was thereby endorsed.

From a letter written by Pope Paul VI after the issuing of *Humanae Vitae* one surmises that a major concern for him was to shore up the traditional sexual ethic against the forces which threatened it. Consistency in principle was crucial for this. The quality of the principle has become more parlous over the years as that consistency has become more strained by technical advance in reproductive science and by concern to avoid HIV infection. At the root of the argument for the intrinsic wrongness of contraception comes a question in logic: Is there a category confusion in assigning to the physical pattern of a biological function the status of a determining moral criterion? That remains a key question for moralists. The *sensus fidelium* does not understand why.

One regrets that the case for natural family planning has been compromised by promoting it as the Catholic answer to contraception. It has value in its own right. It should inspire respect for new life as coming into being in dependence on God as Creator and Father. It should promote mutual understanding between a couple and commit them to positive support for one another. It should build up a sense of co-responsibility between parents in the role of bringing their child into the world. Those who instruct on the use of methods of natural family planning are very aware that it is and must be more than a technique. The values which inspire it secure its human meaning. In this regard John Paul II has said that use of methods of natural family planning may be contraceptive in intent where the motivation is selfishly closed to the responsibility of welcoming new life. What should measure the moral character of the method employed are the moral values that inspire it and which it endorses.

As the years roll on, one comes to appreciate the concern of Paul VI to shore up the traditional sexual ethic. In spite of good intentions, the turmoil that resulted from *Humanae Vitae* has eroded the credibility of that ethic on a broader front. On the basis of general pastoral experience, we need to rethink our approach so as to instil a sense of respect for the intrinsic meaning of human sexuality. This is a crucial challenge. Currently the system of principles that underpinned the traditional structure is in free fall. The current challenge requires more than reformulating the old norms in new terms. What is needed is the voice of a prophet rather than the craft of a moralist, a prophet who will reveal the values behind the norms and respond to what is in the hearts of people who recognise moral truth.

In this context I recall the inspiring words of John Paul II in his first encyclical *Redemptor Hominis*. 'In this creative restlessness (of the human heart) beats and pulsates what is most deeply human – the search for truth, the insatiable need for the good, hunger for freedom, nostalgia for the beautiful and the voice of conscience' (*Redemptor Hominis* 18). This surely should inspire the formulation and the presentation of any Christian ethic. An authentic sexual ethic should be readily accessible because sexuality is so central in the human psyche, setting the tone for personal development and the pattern of life in the human family. This is one area where the *sensus fidelium* should have a role in identifying what is true, good and beautiful and in helping to establish norms of right behaviour which reflect those insights. In its Declaration on Religious Liberty the Second Vatican Council makes a telling point: 'Truth can impose itself on the human mind only in virtue of truth itself, which wins over the mind with both gentleness and power' (*Dignitatis Humanae* 1).

The manner in which Catholic teaching has raised awareness of social justice as a moral challenge for Christians in the world is exemplary. People generally have been made very conscious of injustice and inequality. They have been motivated to make personal sacrifice to confront and correct what they have come to recognise as abusive situations. Church teaching here has been truly prophetic. In meeting many people of goodwill in one's pastoral day-to-day experience, some such prophetic approach holds the only promise of a convincing sexual ethic. True, of its nature sexual ethic at the level of practice will more directly challenge self-indulgence and self-interest. Those who currently promote the mores and patterns of life that apply in our world will not readily give assent to limitations of choice. At a recent conference in London of people engaged in the media, as reported in *The Tablet*, someone asked whether they personally knew anyone who was on the strict pro-life side! That left the group silent. If we cannot affirm conviction on the need to limit choice here, we are up against the difficulty of proposing moral truth in face of dissenting culture.

Even for people of good will one cannot impose moral rules. Motivation based on understanding is required if the aim is to instil the conviction which drives conscience. It neatly sums up the contrast between invoking power and exercising authority. Here a humbler listening mode will prove more effective.

Appreciation of this has been dearly bought through experience of clerical sex abuse and through criticism of attitudes to it on the part of church authority. At source it was a matter of priests and religious being in a position of trust and power which afforded them a sense of immunity. When evil came to light the concern would have been damage limitation, particularly in regard to scandal. The task now is to restore some reason and balance into how we deal with an issue which carries such an emotional charge. This is where a proactive sensitive pastoral approach to the needs of the various parties is the only way forward to achieve healing. In the crisis, we seem to have shied away from that and have invoked cold clinical procedures which have distanced the church from those in distress and have put to one side discernment in managing those charged with abuse. Child protection is the paramount consideration but even so it must operate in a context of reasonableness. Otherwise everyone loses, primarily children.

At the start I promised an overview of life, ranging from teaching moral theology in Maynooth to serving as a pastor in Mallow. Right through it has been a learning curve with a number of fast forwards, not excluding those challenging days conducting the course in medical ethics in University College Dublin. What one appreciates is that ordinary honest-to-God people have so much to offer in day-to-day moral insight. As the proverbial Kerryman said: 'It's a poor day you put your head in your shirt and won't learn something new.' Whatever about other fields of theology, a listening and learning mode is essential for those who are committed to formulating and implementing a moral code.

CHAPTER ELEVEN

Moral discourse in the Irish classroom

Gráinne Treanor

Introduction
The statement that modern people listen more willingly to witnesses than to teachers, and to teachers because they are witnesses,[1] is generously scattered throughout literature on Catholic education. While the conviction with which these words were uttered may not have changed, it would be difficult to deny that the climate in which they apply is substantially different to that in which they were first uttered.

Limiting ourselves to the situation in Ireland, the past thirty years have seen a sea change in the influence of the institutional church on the lives of individual Catholics, especially younger people. Teachers frequently bemoan the lack of any foundation for religious knowledge among their pupils, because religious practice no longer plays any role in the homes from which many of their pupils come. Even at third level, where students have presumably made a conscious choice to study theology, educators find themselves having to go further and further back to the basics, having accepted that many of those who have made the choice to study their subject are nonetheless ignorant of the rudiments of their faith tradition. And, perhaps more significantly still, when students are informed of those rudiments, there can be no assumption, as might have been made in the past, that they will accept them. While there may be little formal empirical evidence to support it, many teachers of moral theology at third level will testify to the fact that their students no longer accept many of the 'teachings' of the Catholic Church, especially in relation to issues of sexual ethics such as pre-marital sex, contraception and homosexuality. And teachers of liturgy or sacramental theology are under no illusion that the students sitting before them are familiar with their subject matter as a result of

---

1. Paul VI, *Evangelii Nuntiandi* (1975) 41, quoting from an *Address to the Members of the Consilium de Laicis* (2 October 1974.)

years of regular participation in the sacraments, including Sunday Mass, through which the faith might have been assimilated or imbibed in the past.

In the light of such change, this chapter reflects on the role of the classroom in the moral education of young people today. It begins by referring briefly to changes in values and beliefs in Ireland over the past two to three decades. It then considers the role of the classroom in moral education. The remainder of the chapter examines the new Junior and Leaving Certificate Religious Education syllabi, and attempts to identify the effects of these on moral discourse in the classroom. In terms of the title, Moral Discourse in the Irish Classroom, 'discourse' is used in a loose, non-technical sense. It is concerned with what is talked about in the classroom (the content of discourse) and how it is talked about (the approach or method of discourse), as well as how this discourse might be viewed from a theological and educational perspective (a little discourse on the discourse).

Changing values and beliefs
People tend to fall into three categories when it comes to their response to the fact that values and beliefs have changed over the past twenty to thirty years, with one of the most notable changes being the declining influence of the Catholic Church on public and private morality.

There are many who see this change primarily in terms of loss: the loss suffered by the church as people reject or ignore its authority; the sense of individuals and society losing their way, floundering in a world where nothing is absolute and everything is subjective; the loss to the community of a system of beliefs and values which served as a social glue, uniting members of that community in a common vision of what is good.

At the other extreme are those who celebrate this change as something positive, although the reasons for their stance may differ significantly. For example, some will celebrate the manner in which individuals now feel more confident to explore their own morality at a personal level, to become truly responsible, or to 'own' their morality. They will interpret the changes mentioned above in the sort of positive terms used by Linda Hogan, commenting on *Veritatis Splendor*, when she writes that

It is wrong to regard the rejection of traditional moral authorities as exclusively the result of subjectivism. There are many reasons why individuals are relying on their own moral judgements. One of the reasons is that people are beginning to internalise the aspirations of Vatican II, which advocated the articulation of an ethic of responsibility. People are redefining the boundaries between the private domain and public interest. In addition, people are giving voice to the complexities of ethical decisions and are rejecting views that leave no room for exceptions or for compromise. The fact that there is an ever increasing gap between the teaching church and the faithful is also giving people the courage and determination to be more autonomous in their ethical decisions.

The shape and character of Catholic morality are certainly changing. The dominant trend seems to be toward personal autonomy and responsibility and away from adherence to externally imposed norms and principles ... To label it subjectivist and then to condemn it represents a serious misunderstanding of what is in fact the emergence of a renewed ethic of responsibility.[2]

Such a positive analysis is also made by Eoin G. Cassidy, who observes that, 'While accepting many key tenets of modernity the Irish remain a deeply religious people with an increasing sense of responsibility towards themselves and towards others.'[3]

The other members of this second category of people who welcome declining attention to the moral voice of the church are those who might be identified as liberals, although the meaning of that label is not without controversy. In this context, it might be applied to those who believe that no religious tradition should determine or shape the morality of a society. They are of the view that those who wish to adhere to traditional church teaching have the right to do so in the privacy of their own lives, but have no right to promulgate that teaching publicly. They welcome the increasing sense of individual responsibility which has been referred to already, because it releases society from the shackles of religious influence.

2. Linda Hogan, *Confronting the Truth: Conscience in the Catholic Tradition*, London, Darton, Longman and Todd, 2000, 22-23.
3. Eoin G. Cassidy, 'Modernity and Religion in Ireland: 1980-2000', in *Measuring Ireland: Discerning Values and Beliefs*, ed. By Eoin G. Cassidy, Dublin, Veritas, 2002, 41.

The third category into which people might be placed, in an attempt to identify their response to changing values and beliefs, might be better described in more passive terms as lack of response. This may stem from indifference, in that people can be aware of change but not feel strongly about it. Increasingly, however, especially among young people, it may stem from an absence of awareness of change. For such people, the church may be irrelevant to their lives because it has never really touched their lives, at least in relation to anything controversial. They may be among the second generation of people for whom the church has not been a significant moral influence. They do not necessarily reject the church's teaching, at least not in any vociferous sense, because they have not really been exposed to it. They have assimilated aspects of secularism in the same way that previous generations assimilated Catholicism. They do not get het up about the church's attitude towards sexual activity between homosexuals, or pre-marital sexual intercourse, because they know and/or care very little about the church's attitude. They have grown up in a secular culture in which pre-marital sexual intercourse and homosexual relations are no longer truly remarkable. What may be more remarkable for them is the fact that any individual or institution could be so strongly against what they perceive as normal. For example, a seminar discussion with a group of third year undergraduate students revealed that, while all were aware in a broad sense that the church was 'against' contraception, only the mature students (that is, those who entered their degree at the age of twenty four or more) were aware that there was ever a lively controversy about the availability of the contraceptive pill in Ireland. They did not realise that it had only become available in this country in the 1980s and that, up to then, the law in Ireland on this issue was very much in keeping with the teachings of the church. This contrasts greatly with the awareness of those mature students who lived through the controversial times of the 'contraceptive train', when a group of women travelled to Belfast, purchased contraceptives, and challenged the authorities by publicly declaring their purchase to customs officials on their return to Dublin. It contrasts even more with the memories of those who can recall the controversy surrounding *Humanae Vitae* when it emerged in 1968. It is easy to forget that, not only have most undergraduate students not lived through this controversy, but that, increasingly, their theology teachers may not either.

Of course, it is important not to adopt a simplistic view of this latter category. To say that many young people today embrace secularism is not strictly true. Many believe in God and prayer. Most have been baptised and confirmed, and have participated, at some time in their lives, in the sacraments of reconciliation and eucharist. Many have or will be married in the church, and will be anxious that their own children are initiated into the church, although religious reasons might not always be their primary motivation. However, what is less disputable is the fact that, when it comes to morality, young people are making up their own minds, and increasingly coming to different conclusions than those held by the church. So, while in 1981, a European Values Study (EVS) showed that 95% of Irish people believed in God, changing to 96% in 1999 (with figures for the age group eighteen to twenty-six only slightly lower), acceptance of key aspects of Catholic moral teaching fell considerably in the same period. For example, acceptance that abortion is always wrong fell from 74% in 1981 to 51% in 1999, and 30% among the eighteen to twenty-six age group. In an International Social Survey Programme (ISSP), acceptance that premarital sexual relations are always wrong fell from 36% in 1991 to 8% in 1998. In 1999, according to the EVS, 35% of Irish people believed that same sex relationships are always wrong, with a figure of 19% in the eighteen to twenty-six age group. The ISSP showed that, in 1991, 68% accepted that such relationships were wrong, falling to 30% in 1998.[4]

The results of these surveys, and the different responses which changes in values and beliefs evoke, are not insignificant, as they contribute towards a description of the climate in which moral discourse occurs in the Irish classroom – be it at primary, secondary or tertiary level. For good or for ill, moral discourse is no longer occurring in classrooms in which the majority of students eagerly argue in favour of the church's teaching, or blindly and unreflectively accept it, or accept it (or let on to accept it) out of fear of an authoritarian teacher or institution. This has significant implications for third level institutions teaching theology, when one considers that many of their students are en route to becoming teachers of Religious Education, either through concurrent teacher training courses or through the completion of a Higher Diploma in Education upon graduation. One is led to

4. Cassidy, 22, 25.

consider the question of where Religious Education is going, if those who are to teach it no longer accept many of the traditional values they are still expected, by the church at least, to teach. Returning to the theme of the opening reference of this chapter, one is led to consider, on the one hand, if these teachers can be called witnesses, as the church expects them to be and, on the other hand, if teachers of Religious Education should be expected to be witnesses at all.

Related to these questions is the issue of the role of the classroom in the religious education of the young person, and in particular, the role of Religious Education (the classroom subject) in moral education.

The Role of Religious Education

How children are exposed to their faith tradition varies considerably according to the system of education in a state. There are many important features which may be common to different states, including the contribution of the family and the role of parish, where faith is important in a family's life. However, the role of the school may be very significant for children educated in one state, but not in another. Sometimes, one cannot even generalise about a particular state, as the experience of those educated in the state system in one place may be different to that of those educated in a 'faith' school in the same place.

What is clear, however, is that children need to 'learn' how to be moral in order to live in co-operation with other human beings and with their environment, whether or not this learning is linked clearly to any faith tradition, education system, or Religious Education programme. A significant part of parental responsibility entails education in morality. From the time their children are very small, many parents are already teaching them the importance of sharing, trying to help them to settle disputes using non-violent means, teaching them that stealing is wrong, and encouraging them to empathise with others. The schools their children go to need to be structured and to function in a way that is moral. In the broader social sphere, the state, in many ways, contributes towards the moral education of its citizens, at least to the extent that it enforces a minimal degree of morality, usually based on the prevention of harm to others, through its legal system. Education in morals/values is therefore a life-long process which involves many interweaving threads, the classroom being only one of these. What is less clear is the extent (or limit) of the role of the classroom in this moral education.

From its literature on education, and on the Catholic school in particular, it is quite clear that the church sees a significant role for the school in the moral education of young people. While identifying the key roles of parents and church, *Gravissimum Educationis* (Declaration on Christian Education, Paul VI, 1965) nevertheless insists that the school has a special importance, and praises those authorities and societies which, 'bearing in mind the pluralism of contemporary society and respecting religious freedom, assist families so that the education of their children can be imparted in all schools according to the individual moral and religious principles of the families'.(#7) The document sees the Catholic school as one which leads students 'to promote efficaciously the good of the earthly city and also prepares them for service in the spread of the Kingdom of God, so that by leading an exemplary apostolic life they become, as it were, as saving leaven in the human community.'(#8)

In Ireland, historical, cultural and social circumstances have led to a situation in which Religious Education has been taught in schools, and has been taught from a denominational perspective. Responsibility for preparing children for the sacraments of reconciliation, eucharist and confirmation has fallen primarily on the school. In the Catholic Church, preparation for sacraments outside of that preparation done in school has been minimal, and Sunday school, while emerging now in some forms for young children as part of the Sunday liturgy, has not been a significant feature. All this points to a heavy reliance on the school in the religious education of primary school children. This reliance is even heavier at second level, where links between school and parish are less evident.

Whether or not this heavy dependence on the school is a good or bad thing is debatable. It could, perhaps, be argued that, were it not for the provision of the subject of Religious Education, very little religious education would take place, and that it is therefore a good thing. Or it could be argued that the state education system should play no role in the provision of denominational religious education at all. From a religious perspective, one could argue that it is a significant deficit in the church in this country that it has not had a greater role in the religious education of young people, including moral education. Of course, to say the church has not had a significant role needs to be qualified. The church has been heavily involved in the creation of syllabi, resources and teacher training. Prior to the introduction of the new Junior and Leaving Certificate syllabi, the syllabi taught in Catholic schools were identifiably Catholic, and used textbooks and other resources published by religious publishers, with the imprimatur of a Catholic bishop. It usually marked the seasons of the liturgical year in both an academic and practical way. However, the fact that most of this has materialised in the classroom, and not elsewhere as well, means that young people tend to associate such education with the school rather than with the church community, and their religious education stops at the school gate.

No matter where one stands on the issue of whether or not the school should be the primary location of religious education, however, it is important to acknowledge the limits of the school as a locus of religious education, and moral education in particular. Graham Rossiter, in an article which treats of the role of Catholic schools in promoting the spiritual and moral development of pupils, examines a number of personal/spiritual change processes to see what range of mechanisms can bring about change in people's beliefs, attitudes, values and behaviour, and suggests that most of these 'do not normally take place in schools, or if they do, it is to a minimal extent'.[5] He points out that too much is often expected of Religious Education in the spiritual and moral development of pupils, to the neglect of the rest of the curriculum and the role of teachers other than teachers of Religious Education.

Nevertheless, he does identify a number of fundamental changes that are needed. For example, he suggests that syllabi for use in Catholic schools have tended 'to be written predominantly with language and content that are perceived by young people as artificially pious and presumptive of a committed church membership – hence the syllabuses do not stray far from traditional Catholic content. The content outlines of many diocesan syllabuses look just like a seminary curriculum; and I believe this is inappropriate.'[6]

5. 'Catholic Education and Values: The Role of Catholic Schools in Promoting the Spiritual and Moral Development of Pupils', in *REA* 4 (Dublin: Mater Dei Insitute of Education, 2003), 105-131, 105.
6. Rossiter, 121.

While he refers here to the situation in Catholic schools in Australia, his comment has relevance in Ireland too, particularly in the light of the secularisation referred to earlier. He argues that many syllabi have little relevance to the lives of young people, and to the issues which concern them, except insofar as religion might be seen as an interesting phenomenon to study. He argues that:

> To change this situation means including more controversial content in Religious Education. To do this calls for a subtle balance between issues and more formal theological topics. It also needs diplomacy. At present, the religion syllabuses in Catholic schools are presenting a religion that is too 'domesticated'. It is not that every line of the syllabuses has to be issue-oriented. But the present pattern needs to shift more in this direction. Some colleagues seem to be saying 'just give them more theology, scripture and good liturgy'. If only it were that simple. This emphasis may be appropriate for seminaries, but not for today's Catholic schools. I am persuaded by the current situation that a more issue-oriented approach is the direction that would make Religious Education more relevant to the majority of young people. It will not automatically magnetise student interest; neither will it make the teaching easier; but I think it will make for a better Religious Education. Also, I believe it is the best option in the classroom for presenting the case for the church, and for fostering church participation.[7]

Rossiter goes on to identify a number of characteristics of this issue-oriented approach. These include systematic study of the issues, limited treatment (in terms of time and depth) which does not compromise the integrity of the subject matter, open, inquiring study, respect for student freedom, the provision of student resources, and a systematic code of teaching ethics. He also refers to two characteristics which are of great significance in terms of the moral development of the pupils. These are, firstly, hopes for personal change and, secondly, avoiding presumption and not requiring personal responses. Of the former he says:

> While there may be a contextual 'hope' that students will appropriate particular values and beliefs (those formally proclaimed by the school), and will take up committed social action, the purpose of teaching and learning related to

7. Rossiter, 122.

contemporary issues is primarily to help them become well informed critical thinkers. What personal stance and social action they eventually take will be influenced by many personal factors outside the classroom – not least of which is the free will of the students themselves.[8]

Of the latter he says

The teaching/learning environment (a type of public forum, even in the church-related school) should not presume beliefs or commitments in students, or that these should be expressed in class; if there is a climate where personal beliefs and commitments are freely discussed, then this is valued for the sensitive contribution that it makes to the learning – but such contributions are not required.[9]

There is a lot to be said for Rossiter's suggestions, especially insofar as they refer to moral education. Even at third level, it is clear to teachers of moral theology that what captures student interest is the exploration of issues such as euthanasia, assisted reproduction, abortion, crime and punishment (including the death penalty), homosexuality, pre-marital sex, etc. Of course, it is difficult to deal adequately with these issues without having already treated of more fundamental themes, such as conscience, natural moral law, the teaching authority of the church, the autonomy of morality and the significance of faith to one's moral vision. However, Rossiter is not calling for an exclusively issues-based syllabus, but one where the balance is in favour of issues which will be perceived by those being taught as relevant to their lives. What might therefore be needed is moral education which centres around issues, and which provides an understanding of the foundational themes necessary to properly discuss these issues, while sometimes using the discussion of issues to either introduce or elucidate foundational themes. For example, the issue of pre-marital sex could be linked to the theme of conscience, with some foundational study of both conscience and the meaning of sexuality having prepared the way for in-depth discussion of the issue. Or an issue related to social justice, such as crime and punishment, could be linked to the theme of the distinctiveness of Christian morality, with the radi-

---

8. Rossiter, 125.
9. Rossiter, 125-126.

cal demands of discipleship elucidated through discussion of that particular issue, rather than in a more abstract manner.

While this approach might have benefits at third level, its value at second level is also worth considering, especially in the light of the significant changes to Religious Education which are occurring with the introduction of Junior and Leaving Certificate syllabi. Some of the concerns expressed by Rossiter about the perceived relevance to young people's lives of their religious education syllabus, while applied to the Australian system, are of equal relevance in Ireland. Many second level students here are switched off when it comes to Religious Education classes. The reasons for this are complex and inter-linked, but must include the fact that, up to recently, it was one of the few unexamined subjects at the level of state examin-ations, and was therefore often perceived as the 'doss class'. In addition, the fact that religion was an unimportant dimension in their lives outside of school meant that it was not perceived as relevant in the classroom either. Where issues were discussed, and this was often a significant part of senior cycle Religious Education, discussion was not always focused or systematic, and sometimes simply pandered to the interests of pupils to placate them, rather than harnessing those interests to lead the student further in moral discourse. Added to this was the fact that a large number of teachers were not specialists in their sub-ject. It is unsurprising, therefore, that so many students studying theology at third level recall their second level Religious Education classes as being only very vaguely religious, or con-sisting of vague discussion (or video viewing) about moral is-sues, or sometimes even being replaced for weeks at a time with preparation for school plays or state examinations. It is therefore probably fair to say that the quality of moral discourse in the classroom has varied widely in quality. The remainder of this chapter will examine the morality sections of the new Junior and Leaving Certificate syllabi in an attempt to identify what hope they have of renewing moral education in the second level class-room, and whether or not this might have welcome repercus-sions for the study of theology at third level too.

Morality in the Junior and Leaving Certificate syllabi
Having taught second level Religious Education in the Republic of Ireland and Northern Ireland before moving into the third

level sector, it is patently clear to me that having the subject examined formally at state level makes a huge difference to what
happens in the classroom. In fact, I would have to admit that it is
what drove me to make my own move to Northern Ireland in
the first place, having taught at second level in the Republic of
Ireland in the year following graduation. It is not necessarily
that having an examination makes things easier, because while
some things become easier when students are motivated to
work by the prospect of examinations, there is also an added
pressure on the teacher who has to prepare students for such
examinations.

In the area of moral discourse, one of the significant (albeit
not exclusive) effects of an examination syllabus is the need for a
very systematic treatment of issues. The luxury of spending
three times as many lessons as originally planned on a topic because it captures the imagination of students might be more cur-
tailed by the restraints of having to complete a syllabus than
would be the case without an examination deadline. But the
need to enable students to write a piece of coursework on euthanasia, or an examination answer on an issue of social justice,
demands that vague, non-directed discussion, or discussion
without any solid body of content apart from student opinion,
or watching the film *Gandhi* for a week, cannot be the staple of
Religious Education lessons. While one could argue that these
should never be the staple of such lessons in any case, the discipline of examination preparation works for both students and
teachers in increasing the likelihood that what happens in the
classroom when moral issues are discussed contributes significantly towards the moral development of the students. And if
discourse involves, as it must, learning that is more than one-
way (teacher to pupil), then such an approach may also enrich
the life of the teacher at times, especially when discourse treats
of issues that have touched the lives of students but have not yet
effected the teacher directly, such as violence, bereavement,
family conflict, serious illness or disability, etc. (I certainly recall
how much I learned about the ability of young people to cope
with suffering and to reach out to those who have been bereaved
when a group of fourteen year olds were faced with the sudden
death of one of their class.) In addition, there is a sense that,
when something is studied for examination, it is often explored
more thoroughly than when it is not examined, with the result

that, whether or not students accept or reject an aspect of religion, examination students at least tend to have a better understanding of what it is they are accepting or rejecting.

So, having nailed my colours to the mast in relation to my stance on examined Religious Education, it is time to briefly assess how morality is treated in the Junior and Leaving Certificate syllabi, and whether or not the manner in which it is treated is a good thing for Irish moral discourse in the classroom.

The aims of Junior and Leaving Certificate Religious Education reflect the overall aims of education as recognised by the Department of Education. It is not possible to describe them in detail here, but the occurrence of the following terms and phrases should give a good sense of what they are about: holistic development; self-awareness; the experience of the spiritual and the human search for meaning; appreciation of the richness of the major religious traditions; engagement with the secular response to human experience; opportunities for reflection on human experience, as well as for understanding and interpretation of that experience; exposure to the non-religious interpretation of life; an informed and critical understanding of the Christian tradition; provision for the moral development of students; critical engagement with moral systems in an effort to arrive at a thought-through moral stance.[10]

The Junior and Leaving Certificate syllabi are best understood as a continuum, with the Leaving Certificate building on and exploring more deeply what has been introduced at Junior Certificate level. In this vein, the Junior Certificate introduces students to ideas such as what it means to be moral, the consequences of actions, the variety of influences on human behaviour, the concept of a moral vision (including religious moral vision), the role of authority and law (including, at higher level, the relationship between state law and religious morality), moral growth, conscience, moral decision making, the influence of religious moral decisions and religious visions of moral failure. While the overall course 'makes particular reference to the Christian tradition, acknowledging the unique role of this tradi-

---

10. An Roinn Oideachais agus Eolaíochta, *Leaving Certificate Religious Education Syllabus, Ordinary and Higher Levels*, 3.

tion and its denominational expressions in Irish life',[11] much of
Section F (*The Moral Challenge*), which is compulsory for those
taking the subject, is not specifically Christian, and in Part 4, students are required to examine 'how two different religious
moral visions contribute to the decision-making of believers
through exploring particular moral decisions and issues'.[12]

It is worth noting that, in the Leaving Certificate syllabus, the
corresponding section (Section D: *Moral decision-making*) is not
compulsory, although issues of morality are not ignored elsewhere. For example, Section A deals with the search for meaning and values, which is not unrelated to morality. Section E
looks at religion and gender, and Section F at issues of justice
and peace, which includes religious perspectives (from a number of traditions) on justice and peace in general, and on specific
issues such as the environment. While morality in the Christian
tradition is explored through an examination of themes such as
the context of the covenant and the Decalogue, the ethical vision
and teaching of Jesus, Christian perspectives on the relationship
between religion and morality, and the Christian understandings of sin and reconciliation, there is also a requirement to
study some of these from the perspective of one tradition other
than the Christian one.

While it is important to acknowledge that, overall, both the
Junior and Leaving Certificate syllabi do devote some sections
specifically to the Christian tradition, if even only because it has
been and continues to be the predominant tradition in Ireland, it
is also important to acknowledge that it is more neutral and less
catechetical than previous programmes. Its tone is more the
pragmatic one of opening students to the phenomenon of religion, examining how this manifests itself in different traditions,
and how religion has shaped and continues to shape communities and individuals at various levels, including the level of
morality. It is notable that the morality section of the Leaving
Certificate refers to Jesus of Nazareth, a title which emphasises
his actual identity as a historical figure, rather than one which
implies faith or confers divinity (as might Jesus Christ.)[13] While
it is not perhaps as issue-based as Rossiter's views suggest

11. An Roinn Oideachais agus Eolaíochta, *Junior Certificate Religious
Education Syllabus (Ordinary and Higher Level)*, 4.
12. *Junior Certificate*, 42
13. *Leaving Certificate*, 44.

might be good for religious education, it is also a far cry from the domesticated, seminary style of education of which he is critical (for its perceived remoteness from the real life of students).

How one reacts to this less catechetical, more neutral approach to Religious Education will probably reflect to a considerable extent the category into which one falls in relation to the declining influence of the Catholic Church on morality in this country (and further afield). If one bemoans the loss of influence as a sign of individualism and relativism, then one probably sees the change in approach to religious education in terms of loss too: the loss to young people of the voice of the church in the classroom; the loss to the church of the one major platform it had from which to address young people on moral issues. If one sees the loss of influence of the church in more positive terms, in the sense of people becoming more individually and reflectively responsible for their morality, then one may welcome the less prescriptive, more open manner in which Christian morality is presented in the classroom. If one falls into the liberal category, which rejects the right of religious traditions to impose their stance through the education system, through state law, etc., one will welcome the more neutral approach of the syllabi, and the fact that reference is made to different religious traditions and to non-religious worldviews, although one might still consider that too much space is given to the Christian tradition, even if it is not in a catechetical mode. If one falls into the more indifferent category, one might not care at all, or one might be spurred into interest because of the relevance to human experience of the study of morality as part of the search for meaning and values.

Perhaps more significant, however, is the potential for the new approach to address the second cohort of the third category referred to earlier, that is, young people who are not so much indifferent out of conscious choice (if that is not an oxymoron), but because they have not really been exposed to true religious education at all, due to the fact that they are second generation lapsed Catholics, and/or because the quality of their religious education has been poor. For them, the new approach represents an opportunity to explore morality as something that is relevant to their lives because it appeals to things that are part of most human being's experience: the influence of parents and communities on morality; the process of moral decision making; the experience of moral failure, the experience of moral dilemmas at an individual and social level, etc. Presented in this more phenomenological way, it is no longer couched in a vocabulary that is alien to its audience (as Rossiter's observations suggest is often the case in existing programmes), and it no longer presupposes a faith commitment that is often not there. It is therefore less likely to be dismissed without consideration as just more of the church pushing its opinion down students' throats. Of course, how one teaches the subject will have some bearing on how it is received. A subject well taught is usually well received, but the converse is also true. In addition, there is scope for religious traditions (already availed of by the Catholic Church) to develop their own guidelines for teachers as to how to go about teaching in a way which links the new syllabi to that tradition. Nevertheless, the overall aims and content of the syllabi suggest a neutrality and breadth which have the potential to give students the opportunity to think about religion more deeply than before, and to consider its role in their lives. It presents morality in an objective way which may evoke personal involvement, but which does not presuppose it. Whether or not students make a link between this and their faith community outside of the school is another matter. That will depend on a number of factors, including the depth of reflection to which the student goes (deep reflection that has a personal impact, or study simply to get points for college admission), the quality of teaching, the conviction of the teacher, and the experience of faith community that the student has outside of school. On the whole, therefore, I would be of the opinion that the Junior and Leaving Certificate syllabi are formulated in a way which has the potential to have a very positive influence on the way in which religion in general, and morality in particular, is understood by young people.

Such a stance is not without its problems, however, considering that the main vehicle for catechesis has, up to now, been the school, even if pupils were not very receptive of that catechesis, and even if not all teachers were convinced about it themselves. This means that the church itself must recognise the limitations of the school and reclaim its catechetical responsibilities if it wishes to continue to catechise. Perhaps it is better, in a more secular society, that catechesis does not continue to depend too much on the classroom, and that, in the classroom, morality is presented in a way that is perceived as less catechetical, when the foundation on which that catechesis might be based is not in place. But the implication of this is that the church has to play its part in parish catechesis, and this is not an easy task, in the light of the reduction in the numbers of clergy and the as yet patchy use of lay resources. There are certainly examples elsewhere (e.g. in the United States) of how this can work, with much effort and co-ordination, but it has yet to materialise in any significant way in this country.

To some, the above assessment of the vision and potential outcomes of the new syllabi might seem like a betrayal, coming as it does from one involved in the teaching of moral theology to students preparing for roles including that of Religious Education teacher. It might also seem like a call to divorce school from parish. I would prefer to see my assessment as a cautious acceptance of reality in relation to what does and does not work in the classroom, in the light of the wider cultural climate in which moral discourse in the classroom takes place. It is also a recognition of the limits of the school and education system, and of the need for the church to recognise these limits for the good of education. And while these might seem to be somewhat negative reasons for this assessment (that is, we must offer this because things have got so bad that nothing else will work), it can also be seen as a positive response in a more secular society, in which it is probably burying one's head in the sand to assume that the traditional catechetical approach, even when well done, will always work. In addition, it can be seen as a recognition of the actual responsibilities of a church which is in need of catechetical revival for both children and adults, in a context in which reliance on the school system may have led to inaction in the past.

The establishment of a comprehensive programme of catechesis at parish level will not be without its problems. It will cost money, require commitment and flexibility from employer and employee, and demand an effort on the part of those who are to participate that was not there when catechesis was simply part of one's school timetable and finished when one finished school. But it is also an opportunity for renewal, and for the development of something which should be regarded as essential but which has often been neglected, that is lifelong education in faith. The idea of moral discourse in the classroom needs to encompass an understanding of classroom in the wider sense as any arena of learning. If, in the larger scale of things, life as a whole is this arena, then moral education cannot end when school ends and, if the church wants to have a voice in ongoing moral education, it needs to establish the framework in which this can take place, whether or not schools continue to play a significant part.

Conclusion
As schools begin to follow the Junior and Leaving Certificate syllabi, the implications for third level education in the area of morality have yet to unfold. One can at present only surmise as to the knock-on effects, if any, for third level. Looking at the situation from one perspective, one might surmise that students coming to study theology at third level will be more informed in the area of morality. Looking at it from another perspective, one might surmise that these students will be more informed in an objective sense, but will not be coming to third level study with any deeper a faith commitment than previously (and possibly less so), because religion and moral traditions have been presented to them as nothing more than different, equally valid ways of interpreting life experience, but lacking any real sense of objective truth. So while third level institutions might benefit from a more informed intake of students, they too need to work out how to address the fact that their institutions, often modelled even more on the seminary model than second level religious education (and often having sprung, academically and physically, from seminaries), may be assuming a commitment that is not there for all the reasons that existed before, but also because the system at second level may not any longer attempt to nurture faith commitment as it did previously.

If the study of theology is not to become a more objective study of religion (mirroring what is happening at second level), in which case one could argue that it is no longer properly called theology, then this means that third level institutions need to engage in catechesis too. This involves paying attention, not only to the strictly academic, but also to the spiritual development of students. While this applies to theology in the broad sense, it also applies more specifically to the way in which morality is treated within theology. It is unlikely, judging from the evidence put forward in this paper, and from common sense observation, that students are going to become suddenly more loyal to traditional church teaching on moral issues once they become theology students. The implications of this are serious, considering how many of these students will in turn become religious educators. If we expect teachers of Religious Education to be catechists and to see their job as one of ministry, then the numbers of candidates who can sincerely accept that ministry will be very small. (That is, unless the church's stance on many issues were to suddenly change and become acceptable to a greater number of those who study them, a compromise which is hardly likely to occur, although the fact that so many reject teachings on particular issues may hint at a need to re-examine and re-present these teachings in a more acceptable way, while at the same time remaining faithful to tradition.) Perhaps it is then safer for the church to stop expecting teachers to be witnesses to what it preaches, if that is to make hypocrites out of many teachers, and to accept that a less faith-based programme in schools will at least allow those teachers to teach without being hypocritical, in a manner that nevertheless awakens students to the meaning of morality. Some might see this as a defeatist attitude; others might see it as a sensible adaptation to the current climate. But adaptation has always been the determining factor as to who or what survives the process of evolution. If adaptation is the key to survival, then it is worth considering.

CHAPTER TWELVE

A discourse on Thomas More's Great Matter: Conscience

D. Vincent Twomey SVD

Poised at the end of the medieval period and the beginning of the modern era, More's understanding of conscience, it is suggested in this essay, belongs to the former theological tradition which the secularised modern era has almost eradicated from our consciousness. This causes some considerable difficulty for us moderns when we attempt to uncover what conscience actually meant for the Lord Chancellor, or indeed when we try to understand the history of this extraordinary man and interpret his writings. This essay is an attempt to explore such methodological difficulties involved in interpreting More and his writings today, before proposing a more comprehensive (ontological) understanding of conscience in order better to understand More himself, in particular his death. To test the validity of this interpretation, the paper applies this fuller notion of conscience to the Utopia, with special reference to the passage on moral philosophy, which, it has been remarked, 'is in fact the cornerstone of the Utopian edifice' (Logan and Adams). Not least because of Patrick Hannon's unique background in English literature and legal studies, this essay on Sir Thomas More, man of letters and lawyer supreme, is offered as a tribute to my colleague in honour of his 65th birthday.*

* * *

More's first formal biographer, described his hero as 'our noble new Socrates'. The parallel is obvious, Chambers adds,[1] noting that Cardinal Pole had first drawn the parallel three years after More's death. Today we call them men of conscience, though Socrates would have asked, what do you mean by that term. And Thomas More would have been not a little amused at our

* I wish to acknowledge my gratitude to Ms Clare Murphy, *Moreanum*, Angers, for her most useful suggestions re the relevant literature on St Thomas More, and also to my colleague, Thomas Canon Finan for his own suggestions, for his careful reading of the manuscript, and for his encouragement.
1. R. W. Chambers, *Thomas More*, London 1935 [1948 reprint], 16.

attempt, or rather attempts, for there are many, to say what conscience is. It is doubtful if any of our answers would have made much sense to him, as indeed they don't seem to make too much sense to us. That is precisely our quandary today. What conscience is, is not so obvious any more.

A useful, though inadequate, definition of conscience is given in Lacoste's *Dictionnaire critique de théologie*, namely, the interior guide that approves or disapproves one's actions. Though implicit in the ancient tragedians and adumbrated in Aristotle's *phronésis*, the notion of conscience was first faintly articulated only by the Stoics.[2] The nearest equivalent in the Old Testament is the notion of the 'heart', a fairly vague notion, also found in the New Testament. Though not a central concept in his writings, St Paul uses the term occasionally. What the New Testament provided, however, was an entirely new context symbolised by personal faith, and martyrdom, as summed up in the words of St Peter (Acts 5:29): 'We must obey God rather than men.' And so, beginning with Origen in the East and Augustine in the West, the Stoic notion was transformed into the uniquely Christian concept it became in the High Scholastic period. One of the most potent influences on that development was the daily examination of conscience. It was central to monastic life, and indeed was not absent from Christian piety in general, forming, as it still does, an essential component of the practice of auricular confession, what one author calls 'the ultimate court of conscience'.[3] By the time we get to the sixteenth century, conscience seems to be on everyone's lips. Beginning with King Henry's scruple about the validity of his marriage, most of the protagonists in More's story at one stage or another appeal to their conscience, including Luther, with whom a new understanding began to emerge, one which has had ramifications down to our own day.

---

2. Cf article on 'Conscience' by John Webster, in *Dictionnaire critique de théologie*, under the general editorship of Jean-Yves Lacoste, Paris (Presse Universitaires de France) 1998, 256; the earliest reference to the Greek term *syneidesis* is found in Democritus (460-c. 357 BC).

3. John A. Guy, 'Law, Equity, and Conscience in Henrician Juristic Thought' in Gordon, J. Schochet (ed), *Reformation, Humanism, and 'Revolution'*, [= The Folger Institute for the History of British Political Thought, Proceedings, Vol I] (Washington, DC, 1990), 1.

Thomas More stood at the watershed that separates the medieval from the modern period. His understanding of conscience was that of the former. We are, in a sense, products of the latter. And part of our difficulty in trying to understand Thomas More is due to our own notion of, or, rather, in the plural, our notions of what constitutes conscience. One could express the difference, rather crudely, by saying that for More conscience was the desire and capacity to know what is the truth of things and their demands on us, both practical and speculative; on the other hand, for many contemporaries conscience is my own personal conviction, opinion or even my deepest feeling. More sought objective truth. We prize our own subjective opinions.

Anthony Kenny, in his extended essay on More, has an instructive discussion of More's understanding of conscience. Central to that discussion is the scholastic theory of an erroneous conscience, namely that one had to act on one's conscience even though it may be in error, provided that one had made sufficient effort to 'inform' one's conscience. Kenny notes that this is the basis of More's defence: he told Cranmer that it was against his conscience to swear the oath since he had informed his conscience. 'But,' Kenny adds, 'for the More in Bolt's play what matters is not whether the Pope's supremacy is true, but the fact that More has committed his inmost self to it. As he says to Norfolk, "What matters to me is not whether it's true or not, but that I believe it to be true, or rather not that I believe it but that *I* believe it".'[4] Now, of course, that is precisely what More

---

4. Anthony Kenny, *Thomas More* [Past Masters Series] (Oxford, 1983), 95. This would seem to be the way some contemporary moral theologians also interpret conscience and even appeal to Bolt's play in support (cf Richard M. Gula SS, *Reason Informed by Faith: Foundations of Catholic Morality* [New York, 1989], 133-5.) By way of contrast, Joseph Koterski SJ, in his preface to *Saint Thomas More: Selected Writings* [Vintage Spiritual Classics], eds John F. Thornton and Susan B. Varenne (New York, 2003), xi-xii, shows how wrong-headed is Bolt's understanding of More's motivation: 'The modern understanding of conscience presumes that one must select one's principles. Being conscientious, then, means remaining consistent with whatever principles one has chosen, as if there were something self-sufficient about an individual's choice of principles and as if any subsequent judgements faithful to those principles must be respected independently of any objective morality. In certain ways this modern position on conscience may be historically rooted in the emphasis given to the supremacy of individual judgement by some Protestant denominations. But under no circumstances should it be mistaken for More's notion of conscience.'

would never have said, not because it has distinct echoes of Luther's *Hier stehe ich, ich kann nicht anders*, but because it is a thoroughly modern concept of conscience, alien, I vouch to claim, to all that More stood, and fell, for.

But the problem of interpreting Thomas More is even more complex. All the terms he uses in his moral philosophy or theology are indeed still in use, but they no longer have the meaning or resonance they would have had for More or those who inspired him, in particular Thomas Aquinas. To take one term: the central concept of 'virtue'. Already in the late seventeenth century the broader term 'moral' is used in its most restricted sense of all, that which has to do primarily with sexual behaviour.[5] By the nineteenth century, colloquial speech had confined the term virtue exclusively to the sexual sphere. One could say that the phrase 'a woman of low virtue' marks its nadir. Despite a recovery of the classical notion of virtue in recent decades, a renowned contemporary moral theologian could write (very persuasively) about compassion as 'the virtue of our age'.[6] Such a loose usage of the term would have puzzled any scholastic, since compassion is not a virtue, but an emotion, at best one of those passions which need to be moulded into the virtues of fortitude and temperance, sometimes by resisting them at their most intense pitch.

In *After Virtue*, Alasdair MacIntyre, as is well known, noted that contemporary public debate is characterised primarily by interminable disputes. This he maintains is due to the lack of an agreed moral language. 'The most striking feature of contemporary moral utterance is that so much of it is used to express disagreements; and the most striking feature of debates in which these disagreements are expressed is their interminable character.'[7] His study of the history of ethics led him to the insight that he describes in terms of a grim parable, which Sachs summarises as follows:

Imagine, he says, that at some time in the future there is a

---

5. Alasdair MacIntyre, *After Virtue, A Study in Moral Theory*, (London, 1981), 37.

6. Oliver O'Donovan, *Begotten or Made?* (Oxford, 1984), 11. I should add that, apart from the possibly ironic use of the term 'virtue' in this context, I am otherwise fully in agreement with his main thesis, which is that emotion not reason seems to determine moral action in the modern world.

7. Ibid., 6.

widespread revolution against science. There is a series of ecological disasters. Science and technology are blamed. There is a public panic. Riots break out. Laboratories are burned down. A new political party comes to power on a wave of anti-scientific activity. A century later, the mood subsides. People begin to try to reconstruct what was destroyed. But all they have are fragments of what was once a coherent scientific culture: odd pages from all books, scientific instruments whose use has been forgotten, bits and pieces of information about theories and experiments without the background of knowledge of their context. These pieces are reassembled into a discipline called science. Its terminology and some of its practices resemble science. But the systematic corpus of beliefs which once underlay them has gone. There would be no unitary conception of what science was about, what its practices were for, or what its key terms signified. The illusion would persist that science had been recovered. But it would have been lost, and there would be no way of discovering that it had been lost.[8]

The philosophical endeavour of the Enlightenment, which he calls the secularisation of Protestantism, was the beginning of various efforts to reconstruct a moral system made up of the fragments left over from an earlier revolt against the classical system of medieval Europe. The main object was to find a moral justification for values needed to preserve a minimum of order in society. Each effort to find a philosophical justification for morality failed – as it was bound to fail – until eventually emotivism prevailed, as it does to a large extent today in our Western culture. This is, put simply, the denial that in the sphere of morality there is any such thing, strictly speaking, as objectivity. Morality is essentially irrational feeling, personal preference.

MacIntyre does not simply describe the moral debris, or its origins. He tries to recover the original, classical science of morality based on the Greek notion of *areté*, usually inadequately rendered as virtue. It is a term that defies translation, as Professor Thomas Canon Finan has pointed out. The closest English equivalent might be 'human excellence and goodness'. We will return to it.

This has implications for interpreting Thomas More, in particular since he seems to have been one of the first victims of that

8. Jonathan Sacks, *The Politics of Hope*, (London, 1997), 32

revolution which eventually swept away the moral language in the light of which he understood his own life and philosophy, and which would have allowed us to understand him. It follows that conscience, whatever it is, cannot be understood in isolation; it is part of a system of thought and life, personal and communal, central to which is virtue as the context of all moral discourse.

Witness to Conscience

This raises the interesting question as to whether or not we moderns can ever really grasp what More understood by conscience.[9] One might argue that sufficient common ground still exists for most people of upright lives to recognise and respond to Thomas More's unique character and integrity (both products of virtue), in particular his readiness to sacrifice everything for what he in conscience held to be, not simply his opinion (Plato's *doxa*), but truths of universal validity (*theória*). But that answer is not entirely convincing. The real reason why it is possible to recover 'More's conscience', as it were, will I hope become clear in an attempt to do precisely that. Let us begin by glancing at his life and one of his writings.

As one author has demonstrated, More's life and writings give us a unique insight into the way he came to those momentous decisions that marked his life and changed history.[10] He battled for four years with the question of his vocation, monastic life or marriage, before opting for the latter. His crisis of conscience when invited to enter the Royal service is documented dramatically in that wonderful dialogue between Raphael

---

9. One of the most impressive accounts of More's understanding of conscience is that penned by the great More scholar, André Prévost, 'Conscience and the Ultimate Court of Appeal' in R. S. Sylvester and G. P. Marc'hadour (eds), *Essential Articles for the study of Thomas More* (Hamden, Conn., 1977), 563-8. See also the account by Brian Byron in his *Loyalty in the Spirituality of St Thomas More*, (Nieukoop, 1972), 38-42. Modern readers will find it difficult to assimilate these accounts, not because of any inability on the part of the authors – on the contrary – but rather because of the assumptions we moderns bring to our reading of it; see, for example the quotation below in footnote 13.
10. See Chamber, op. cit, *passim*. For a succinct and more complete account of the following, see Rudolf B Gottfried's article, 'A Conscience Undeflowered' in Sylvester and Marc'hadour, *Essential Articles*, op. cit., 520-38.

Hythlodaeus and More in Book I of *Utopia*.[11] His attitude to the papal supremacy was the product of some ten days vigorous research as a result of a question posed by Antonio Bonvisi. His decision not to sign the Oath of Supremacy and to remain silent on the King's Great Matter caused him many sleepless nights, as he pondered the consequences for his wife, asleep at his side, and his beloved family all around him, before he could say to a bewildered Roper, immediately after leaving Chelsea for the last time: 'Son Roper, I thank our Lord, the field is won.'[12] He had made his conscientious decision, having counted the cost. In each of these momentous decisions, More demonstrated what Aquinas meant when he said that conscience is our participation in the providence of God, when each of us becomes a lawmaker for ourselves.[13]

It is noteworthy that all his major personal decisions were marked by self-renunciation. At the request of his father, he

---

11. See Gottfried, op. cit., 525-6.

12. Chambers, op. cit., 301. Prévost comments: 'Although conscience represents an outstanding value which cannot be "made captive," it is nonetheless dependent upon *objective reality*. Therefore such conscience is not the fixed idea of an obstinate man who will not listen to reason. Before coming to a conclusion which imposed itself to his conscience, More submitted himself to a tremendous amount of homework. And even after forming his conscience, he still acknowledged two authorities that could prevail against his own conclusions: the decrees of a General Council or the unequivocal expression of the "common faith" of the universal church, which, in his opinion, have received from God the power of expressing revealed truth' (Prévost, op. cit., 567).

13. 'Conscience for [More] is an absolute, his own and no one else's concern; no man has a right to exert any pressure whatsoever on it; so highly does he value it that he will offer his life in order to remain true to it. Individual conscience stands above all opinions. It knows no other rule than itself, God and God's will: "But as concerning mine own self, for thy comfort shall I say, daughter, to thee, that mine own conscience in this matter (I damn none other man's) is such as may well stand with mine own salvation; therefore am I, Meg, as sure as that God is in heaven"' (Prévost, op. cit., 566; quotation from Rogers, op. cit., 528). The extraordinary dialogue between More and Margaret in the Tower as reported by his daughter in her 1534 Letter to Lady Alice Allington – Chambers compares the letter to Plato's *Crito* –, the term 'conscience', according to G. Marc'hadour, occurs at least forty four times (text in *The Correspondence of Sir Thomas More*, edited by Elizabeth Frances Rogers [Pincetown, 1947] letter 206, 514-32). It is well summarised by Prévost (see above, especially footnote 12).

gave up Oxford and letters for New Inn and law. In deference to the grief he might cause the elder sister of the Colt family, he chose Jane as his first wife rather than the younger sister he really fancied. Just as he was coming into his own as a star among the European humanists, he sacrificed a brilliant literary future, fame, and whatever academic freedom he might have enjoyed, in order to enter into the service of the King. Having no thirst for polemics, he entered the theological fray when requested by the English bishops. Eventually he sacrificed his property, his wife, family, friends and even life for the *unum necessarium* and thought all else as nought. His decisions of conscience were modelled on the *kenosis*, the self-emptying of Christ, as taught in his favourite devotional writings, *The Imitation of Christ*. The hair-shirt was his daily reminder of submission to the will of the Father. In all this More was acutely aware that he was being sustained by that ineffable thing we call grace, that mysterious presence of the love of God poured into our hearts that draws us to union with him. To understand More's conscience, one has to keep both these things in mind: Christ as More's exemplar and Christ as the source for living according to that exemplar. In the Tower, he returns over and over again to the Passion and composes his treatise on the sufferings of Christ. In a word, his decisions of conscience were his attempt to know and do not his own will but the will of God. His life of prayer and union with God are also the source of the care-free joy and liberating wit that marked his every word and deed, right up to the moment of his execution. He summed up his whole life in his final words: 'I die the King's good servant, [but] God's first.'

As a lawyer, particularly later as a judge and Lord Chancellor,[14] More's fairness and justice would seem to have been based on his attempt to know the truth of each case before him and to see beyond the letter of positive law to the spirit, the origin of the notion of equity, central to medieval English juris-

---

14. 'The Chancery was the great secretarial bureau: a Home Office, a Foreign Office, a Ministry of Justice. It was the centre of the English legal system and the political centre of the Constitution. The Lord Chancellor was the highest rank of the King's servants, "the King's natural Prime Minister". He acted as Secretary of State for all departments, and was Keeper of the Great Seal which was, in Matthew Paris' phrase, the key to the kingdom' (Richard O'Sullivan QC, *The Inheritance of the Common Law*, The Hamlyn Lectures, Second Series, [London, 1950], 110).

prudence.[15] The ancients called this acquired disposition the virtue of prudence, the highest in rank of, and the precondition for, all the other virtues. If the object of law is justice, then the precondition for justice is to know not simply the legal complexities of a case and the details of the relevant laws, written and unwritten, but the truth about the particular situation involved in each case, before a just judgement could be made. And indeed what modern theologians often refer to as conscience – the ability to judge what one ought to do in a particular situation after one has 'informed' one's conscience – would have been seen by the ancients as an aspect of prudence, *phronésis*.[16] One of the characteristics of prudence is the acquired disposition to get to the heart of the matter swiftly and with a sure touch. The technical terms for this is *sollertia*, which is a '"perfected ability" by virtue of which man, when confronted with a sudden event … can swiftly, but with open eyes and clear vision, decide for the good, avoiding the pitfalls of injustice, cowardice, and intemperance.'[17] More's life not only exemplified this *sollertia*. His ability to clear the backlog of cases he inherited from Wolsey and see the day when there were no more cases awaiting judgement is proof that he possessed the virtue of prudence in an eminent degree.[18] After examining the evidence, one author described him as 'a hard-working administrator, a peacemaker more concerned

15. See the article by Richard O'Sullivan quoted in the previous footnote.

16. Nicholas Madden OCD aptly suggested translating *phronésis* as 'imperative discernment'.

17. Josef Pieper, *Prudence*, (London, 1957), 28.

18. See the chapter entitled 'Law and Conscience' in Richard O'Sullivan, op. cit., 93-118, which maps the development of equity in English law in the course of which the practice of earlier Common Law was perfected by the Chancellor's Court's wide use of its discretionary powers. In exercising such powers, judges (following the principle first enunciated by St Thomas Aquinas) were obliged in conscience to judge purely on the objective facts of the case. There O'Sullivan quotes More's son-in-law, Roper, who recalled Thomas's response to judges who objected to the Injunctions he granted. After inviting them to his home, he explained after dinner to them how he came to his decisions. They admitted that they too 'could haue done no other wise themselves'. He added, in Roper's words: 'that if the Iustices of euery courte (unto whom the reformacion of the rigour of the lawe, by reason of their office, most especially appertained) wold, upon reasonable consideration, by their owne discretions (as they were, as he thought, in conciens

to get at the sources of violence in the countryside than to inflict harsh penalties, a protector of the weak against the strong, and an astute lawyer who could cut through a mass of detail to the heart of the matter at hand.'[19]

Another aspect of conscience is courage or, to be more accurate, the virtue of fortitude. It is closely related to the social or communal dimension of conscience and has enormous implications for politics. When the Romans coined the term virtue, perhaps it was this aspect in particular which they had in mind. We see it in the way More managed to secure liberty of expression for parliament when appointed Lord Chancellor, the origin of parliamentary privilege.[20] Democracy is based on free speech which is the prerequisite for a genuine debate leading to a truly prudential decision by the ruler, that dictate of practical reason

---

bound) mitigate and reforme the rigour of the lawe themselves, there should from thenceforth by him no more Iniunctions be granted' (O'Sullivan, op. cit., 109). But More knew that most judges did not want to take that moral responsibility on themselves, though they were in conscience bound to do so. Conscience, taking the particular circumstances into consideration, should modify the law. This primacy of conscience, here understood as *objective* morality, would be challenged by More's contemporary, and religious opponent, Christopher St German, who, in *Doctor and Student* affirmed: 'Forasmuch as it behoveth thee to be occupied in such things as pertain to the law, it is necessary that thou ever hold a pure and clear conscience: and I counsel thee that thou love that is good, and fly that is evil; that thou do nothing against truth: and that thou do justice to every man as much as in thee is; and also that in every general rule of the law thou do observe and keep equity. And if thou do thus, I trust the light of thy lantern, that is, thy conscience shall never be extinct' (as quoted in Lewis Watts, SJ, 'Conscience in Court' in Richard O'Sullivan QC, *The King's Good Servant: Papers read to The Thomas More Society of London*, [Oxford, 1948], 112; see also below, footnote 46, where St German keeps closer to the traditional concept). For a succinct discussion of the Thomistic understanding of relationship between law and conscience, which More shared, see Hilary J. Carpenter OP, 'Law and Conscience' in Richard O'Sullivan, QC, *The King's Good Servant*, op. cit., 49-59.

19. Margaret Hastings, 'Sir Thomas More: Maker of English Law?' in Sylvester and Marc'hadour, *Essential Articles*, op. cit., 118.

20. It is captured most forcibly in what may well be the legend of how Thomas More, the young burgess, challenged King Henry VII and forced him to yield to the parliament's just demands. Legends convey their own truths, which tend to be deeper than empirical truths.

which is law. But few are ever willing to exercise free speech due to fear of intimidation and reprisals. More, it would seem, did so, but only when prudence dictated. More specifically, the virtue of fortitude is manifested in endurance in the face of unavoidable injustice. Martyrdom is the ultimate expression of fortitude as endurance. It is important to recall that More rejected the popular false heroism of the late medieval lives of martyrs, and, following the words of Christ, insisted that given the opportunity one should flee persecution. Martyrdom is not to be sought out, but, when all else fails, it must be accepted as God's will. Theory became practice in his public silence with regard to the King's Great Matter. His writings in the Tower indicate the source of that fortitude: the theological virtue of hope: that one day we will all be merry in heaven. It becomes almost an antiphon in his final days.

Is there any more to be said? Indeed we have not really touched the core of the mystery of conscience. Here I wish to draw on a recent essay on conscience by Joseph Cardinal Ratzinger, conscience being one of the themes that occurs repeatedly in his writings.[21] It is an essay with the revealing subtitle: 'Conscience and Truth'.[22]

The Nature of Conscience
What Ratzinger achieves in this essay, it seems to me, is the recovery of what might be described as the ontological level of conscience. In the Middle Ages it was known as *synteresis* or *synderesis*, a term taken from Stoicism, as distinct from *conscientia*, the level of judgement, i.e. conscience in the narrow sense of the term as up to now in discussing More's life. Ratzinger prefers the more Platonic term *anamnesis* to the Stoic term. It is a term, moreover, that is close to biblical thought, such as St Paul describes in Rom 2:14f: the law that is written into our hearts.[23]

---

21. Cf Vincent Twomey, 'La coscienze e l'uomo' in *Alla scuola della Verità*, (Cinesello, Balsamo, Milan, 1997), 111-45, the following section on the nature of conscience is a slightly revised version of pages 138-43.
22. Most recently reprinted in English translation in *Benedict XVI and Cardinal Newman*, edited by Peter Jennings (Oxford: Family Publications, 2005), 41-52. Quotations from the text given here are my own translation of the German original as printed in Joseph Cardinal Ratzinger, *Wahrheit, Werte, Macht: Prüfsteine der pluralistischen Gesellschaft*, (Freiburg, 1993).
23. The term also has liturgical, sacramental associations.

This ontological level of conscience was first discovered by
Socrates, whom Ratzinger regards almost as a prophet of Jesus
Christ, and was central to tradition from St Basil the Great and St
Augustine to the medieval mystics and the high scholastics, including St Thomas Aquinas.[24] According to Ratzinger it is also
central to the thought of the two great Englishmen, Thomas
More and Cardinal Newman. But in modern post-scholastic
theology it was effectively forgotten,[25] with the consequent
shrivelling of conscience to the second level, that of practical
judgement. This led in our time to two apparently contradictory
but in fact closely related perversions of the notion of conscience, that of the erroneous conscience[26] and that of the infalli-
ble conscience. The former has come to mean in effect that it
does not matter what one does, provided one is sincerely convinced that it is right, while the latter affirms that conscience
cannot err, that what you think is right is in fact right.
Conscience is reduced to an 'excuse mechanism',[27] and so neither Hitler nor Stalin can be condemned. Both notions receive
their persuasiveness, if not their inspiration, from the prevailing
relativism of modernity,[28] the end product of the Enlightenment

24. The Thomistic understanding is well articulated by Alasdair
MacIntyre as 'that fundamental, initial grasp of the primary precepts of
the natural law, to which cultural degeneration can partially or tem-
porarily blind us but which can never be obliterated' (*Three Rival
Versions of Moral Enquiry: Encyclopedia, Genealogy, and Tradition being the
Gifford Lectures delivered in the University of Edinburgh in 1988*, [London,
1990], 194).
25. The great exception here, as usual, was Josef Pieper: cf his *Traktat
über die Klugheit*, (Munich 1949), 23-36 (in the 6th printing in 1960); see
also his book, *Die Wirklichkeit und das Gute*, (Munich 1949). Pieper too
speaks about the presence of an *Ur-Gewissen*, which might be translated
as 'primal conscience'.
26. Here Ratzinger draws attention to the research of J. G. Belmans, 'La
paradoxie de la conscience erronée d'Abélard à Karl Rahner', in *Revue
Thomiste* 9 (1990), 570-586, which demonstrates that, with the appear-
ance in 1942 of Sertillanges book on Thomas, a falsification of Aquinas'
teaching on conscience began which has been widely influential.
27. *Wahrheit, Werte, Macht*, 39.
28. See Peter Fonk, 'Die Kunst des Steuermanns. Aristotles Beitrag zu
einer theologischen Lehre vom Gewissen' in: K. Arntz and P.
Schallenberg (eds), *Ethik zwischen Anspruch und Zuspruch*, (Freiburg
1996), 267-295 for some useful information about the historical origins
of the two notions.

project built on the autonomy of the subject and the absolute claims of reason. It is now floundering in uncritical conformity to convention and the reduction of reason to empirical or quantitative rationality.[29]

Both notions, in a word, reflect that all-pervasive subjectivity which reduces morality to personal preference, something ultimately irrational. 'In such a "relativistic" context,' Ratzinger mentions in an aside, 'teleological or consequentialist ethics [now also the predominant school of thought in moral theology] becomes in the final analysis nihilistic. And when, in such a worldview, one mentions 'conscience' the description for it is – more profoundly considered – that there is no such thing as conscience as such, namely co-knowing with truth. Each one determines his own criteria, and in the general relativity no one can be of assistance to the other, much less make regulations for him ...'[30]

What then is the ontological level of conscience? It is '... the window that opens up to man the view of the common truth that establishes and sustains us all and so makes community of decision and responsibility possible due to the common ground of perception.'[31] Pure subjectivity, on the other hand, disposes of the obligation to search for the truth and removes any doubt about generally accepted attitudes. It suffices to be convinced about one's own views and adjust to the views of others: the more superficial one's views the better. But a firmly subjective conviction untouched by guilt is in fact a symptom of a sickness of the soul.[32] The inability to experience guilt is the sin of the Pharisees.

Interpreting Rom 2:1-16, where Paul undermines the theory of salvation through lack of knowledge of the truth (in other words, due to an erroneous conscience), Ratzinger says:

> There is in man the presence of truth which cannot be disallowed – that truth of the Creator which in salvific-historical

29. cf Joseph Ratzinger, *Church, Ecumenism, Politics. New Essays in Ecclesiology*, trs Robert Nowell (Slough,1988) 153/4; 231-232]; ibid. *Turning Point for Europe?* (San Francisco, 1994), 31-35]; *Wahrheit, Werte, Macht*, 65-73.

30. Ibid., 46.

31. Ibid., 32; see also Joseph Cardinal Ratzinger, *Principles of Catholic Theology* (San Francisco, 1987) 55-57.

32. Ratzinger (*Wahrheit, Werte, Macht*, 34-35) refers to the psychologist A. Görres, 'Schuld und Schuldgefühl', in *Internationale katholische Zeitschrift Communio* 13 (1984), 434.

revelation has also become written down. Man can see the truth of God as a result of being created. Not to see it is guilt. It is not seen, if and because it is not willed. This 'no' of the will which prevents knowledge is guilt. Then the fact that the signal-lamp does not light up is a consequence of an intentional looking away from that which we do not want to see.[33]

According to Newman, who rejected the liberal notion of the subject as a self-sufficient criterion over against the demands of authority in a world devoid of truth, conscience means: '... the audible and imperious presence of the voice of truth in the subject himself; conscience is the cancellation of pure subjectivity in the contact made between the interiority of man and the truth that comes from God.'[34]

The first, as it were, ontological level of conscience, then, consists in the fact 'that something like *a primal memory (eine Urerinnerung) of the good and of the true* (both are identical) is implanted in us; that there is an inner tendency of being in man made in the likeness of God towards that which is in conformity with God ... This *anamnesis* of the origin, which results from that constitution of our being which is in conformity with God, is not a conceptual, articulated knowledge, a treasury of recallable contents. It is, as it were, an interior sense, a capacity of re-cognition, so that the person who is thereby addressed, and is not opaque within, recognises the echo of it in himself.'[35] St Augustine formulated it more simply as the sense for the good that is imprinted in us.[36] However, this sense needs, as it were, help from without in order to become itself; what is external to it performs a maieutic function, to bring its own openness for truth to fulfilment. What is outside is the authority of the church[37] – but also presumably includes any genuine moral authority.

With regard to the Christian there is yet another dimension to be mentioned that goes beyond the radius of creation: the *anamnesis* of the new 'we' which has been granted to us through our incorporation into Christ. St John appeals to this Christian memory, that is always learning but which, on the basis of its

---

33. *Wahrheit, Werte, Macht*, 37.
34. Ibid., 43.
35. Ibid., 51-52.
36. cf ibid., 51, 53.
37. cf ibid., 53-54.

own sacramental identity, can distinguish between what is the unfolding of memory and what is its falsification (cf 1 Jn 2:20).[38]

The second level of conscience comes into play in the act of judgement as to what one should do in a particular situation which is always unique. As I have already mentioned above, conscience here would seem to be closely related to the virtue of prudence.[39] Both levels are distinct but interrelated. One must act according to one's judgement, even if it is objectively wrong – but one may be guilty for coming to the wrong decision. The guilt lies somewhere else, not for judging something right that is in fact objectively wrong, but deeper, ' ... in the desolation of my being that makes me insensible for the voice of truth and its appeal to my inner self.'[40] For this reason criminals like Hitler and Stalin are guilty.

There is a final dimension that Ratzinger mentions in an epilogue, that of grace: the forgiveness of God once we recognise our guilt. It is the divine power of expiation, which, as the Greeks already recognised, would be needed to wash away our guilt. Without attention to this, the real core of the Christian message, truth can become a yoke on our shoulders too heavy for us to bear.

The recovery of the ontological level of conscience throws new light on what is meant by that objective morality which, before the modern period, was universally recognised by the wisdom of humanity. That is 'the conviction that man's being contains an imperative, the conviction that he does not himself invent morality on the basis of expediency, but rather finds it already present in things.'[41] This conviction is common to all the great religious and wisdom traditions of humanity, which flow like tributaries into the great Christian vision of reality. 'The ethical vision of the Christian faith is not in fact something specific to Christianity but is the synthesis of the great ethical intuitions of mankind from a new centre that holds them together.'[42]

---

38. Ibid., 54-55.

39. See Josef Pieper, *Traktat über die Klugheit*, op. cit., especially 23-44.

40. Ibid., 58.

41. *Turning Point for Europe?*, 28-29; there Ratzinger takes up and develops the insights of C. S. Lewis, *The Abolition of Man* (Oxford, 1943).

42. *Turning Point for Europe?*, 37; see also his contribution to Heinz Schürmann, Joseph Cardinal Ratzinger, Hans Urs von Balthasar, *Principles of Christian Morality*, trs Graham Harrison (San Francisco, 1986), 43-66.

This understanding of the underlying, ontological basis of conscience, it seems to me, is at the core of More's *Utopia*.

The Utopia of Thomas More

Hythlodaeus concludes his discourse in Book I with a comment on the eagerness of the Utopians to learn what they can from anyone coming from another culture or civilisation: 'This readiness to learn is, I think, the really important reason for their being better governed and living more happily that we do,' Hythlodaeus says, 'though we are not inferior to them in brains or resources,'[43] a jab at European arrogance. Europe was losing the capacity – the humility – needed to learn from others.

Similarly in Book II, Hythlodaeus concludes his account of Utopia and its commonwealth with a description of the content of the Utopians' common worship: they acknowledge God as the creator and ruler of the universe, author of all that is good. They thank him for his benefits, in particular the way of life in the commonwealth and their religious ideas 'which they hope are the truest'. Then Hythlodaeus adds: 'If they are wrong in this, and if there is some sort of society or religion more acceptable to God than the present one, they pray that he will, in his goodness, reveal it to them, for they are ready to follow wherever he leads ....'[44] More here may well be reminding his readers, as some commentators claim, that the supposedly ideal commonwealth is but the product of reason unaided by revelation, which would explain why some of the customs of the Utopians are contrary to Christian practice. But I think that More is drawing his readers attention to something more serious than the questionable practices of, say, female priests, divorce or euthanasia: namely the closing of the European soul in contrast with the humility and openness of the Utopians. That closure resulted from a new relationship of man to reality as expressed in the way Pico della Mirandola presents God as speaking to the first man:

> No domicile, no form, no special task have I given you, O Adam, so that you may choose domicile, form and task for your self and what you choose should be yours according to

43. Thomas More, *Utopia*, edited by George M. Logan and Robert M. Adams, (Cambridge Texts in the History of Political Thought) Cambridge 1989, 41.
44. Ibid., 106.

your mind. All other creatures have I conceived with a particular nature and thus enclosed them within definite boundaries. You are restricted by no narrow limits. According to your will, in whose hand I have given you, you yourself can determine that nature.[45]

No wonder Rome quaked. This divinisation of natural man is the source of all human hubris: unlimited free choice.

The readiness of the Utopians to learn and their openness to correction about their way of life and their religious ideas are but two sides of the one coin, and that coin is conscience, not the second level, prudence, but the first, ontological level.[46] As far as I can ascertain, the term 'conscience', though used by some translators, is not found in the text itself.

Book II is an account of life in Utopia. It begins with a description of the external territory and ends with a discourse on the internal territory of the heart: virtue and religion. Like Plato and Aristotle who provided the main inspiration for Utopia, it

45. *De hominis dignitate* Ioannis Pici Mirandulae, *Opera quae extant omnia*, (Basel, 1601), 208. I am grateful to Ms Penny Woods for locating this book for me in the Russell Library, Maynooth. Isaiah Berlin comments that, like Machiavelli, who 'stressed will, boldness, address, at the expense of rules laid down by calm *ragione*', 'so, too, in his own fashion did Pico della Mirandola in his apostrophe to the powers of man, who unlike the angels, can transform himself into any shape – the ardent image which lies at the heart of European humanism in the north as well as in the Mediterranean' (Isaiah Berlin, *Against the Current: Essays in the History of Ideas*, edited by Henry Hardy with an introduction by Roger Hausheer [London, 1979], 74).

46. It is interesting to note that the distinction between the two levels seems to have been commonplace at this period, if we look at the definition of conscience found in *Dialogue of Doctor and Student* by Christopher St German. He defined it 'as the driving force within the human soul that inclines man to pursue good and eschew evil and which is capable of distinguishing the two at a practical level. Both motive and cognitive in this abstract sense, conscience was an objectivized gauge of ethical evaluation, and it was this gauge that was applied as a theoretical yardstick against the defendant's real-life morality in a particular case in Chancery in order to arrive at a corrective sentence (or decree) should any prove necessary' (Schochet, op. cit., 2). However, St German, it seems, modified the earlier understanding of equity quite significantly: For him, 'Equity was not an absolute, but was to be relative to the common erudition of lawyers. It was therefore human and fallible. In particular, it was vulnerable to the political atmosphere of the Inns of Court at a given historical moment' (ibid., 11).

would seem that the real discovery the fictional traveller made
was not an ideal commonwealth but the perennial truths that
order in society is dependent on order in the soul (virtue), that
virtue is related to transcendence, and that man is the measure
of society because God is the measure of his soul (conscience).
As in the Greek experience, this discovery of what one author
calls the anthropological principle governing society was made
against a background of the dominant cosmological principle.[47]
According to the latter, society, in particular its representative,
the prince, or, more precisely, the emperor, was in turn the ultimate representative of eternal order so that his word was law
and there was no appeal to a higher instance. The Greeks broke
through this concept of order in society to discover the unmea-
sured measure of all law (*Solon*), the unwritten law that mea-
sured the licitness of all human laws (*Sophocles*), the primacy of
transcendent truth that could not be exhausted in any human
law or teaching but could be glimpsed with no small effort by
the just man, whose justice is the fruit of his search for the truth
and whose destiny would be that of Socrates.[48] Thomas More
witnessed in his day the re-emergence of the cosmological principle that placed the prince above morality[49] and so gave him
unlimited power, and god-like status: the so-called divine right
of kings. That emergence was cloaked in the garb of expediency
and thus, for the sake of the presumed greater good, the individual could, and would, be sacrificed. What could not be tolerated

---

47. cf Eric Voegelin, *The New Science of Politics: An Introduction* (Chicago
& London, 1952, reprint 1983), 52-9.

48. cf ibid., 59-75. Voegelin describes this as the anthropological principle, the discovery of the soul as the sensorium of transcendence and
with it the recognition 'that a polis is man written large', to use Plato's
often-quoted phrase. 'A political society in existence will have to be an
ordered cosmion, but not at the price of man; it should be not only a
microcosmos but also a macroanthropos' (ibid., 61).

49. 'Utopia is in part, a protest against the New Statesmanship: against
the new idea of the autocratic prince to whom everything is allowed'
(Chambers, op. cit., 131). Two years before the publication of *Utopia* in
1506, Machiavelli had finished writing his treatise on the New
Statesmanship, *The Prince* (cf George Bull in his introduction to his
translation in the Penguin Books, 1961, 19), which Thomas Cromwell
once offered to lend to Cardinal Pole and which evidently suited
Cromwell's own disposition. 'Parts of *Utopia*', Chambers notes, 'read
like a commentary on parts of *The Prince*' (ibid., 132).

is the man who would give God the primacy over the State,[50] as Thomas More summed up his whole life in his parting words before his execution. 'God first' pithily captures More's fidelity to his conscience: 'the voice of God within', to quote the Second Vatican Council, following Newman.

It has been pointed out[51] that 'The question of the moral and the expedient interested More deeply, as it did other humanists.' And that indeed the account of Utopia is an attempt, among other things, to answer the question: 'Is it possible, even theoretically, for a commonwealth to be both moral and expedient?'[52] This may indeed be true, but it strikes me as somewhat scholastic, using the term in the somewhat pejorative sense that More used it. Is it possible that what preoccupied More was the more radical question: would morality survive the triumph of the expediency he could observe near and far, where increasingly men were using human laws to set aside the law of God[53] just as preachers adjusted the teaching of Christ to suit the wishes of men?[54] Morality itself was being redefined as utility and so its

---

50. 'More's trial turned on the Erastian question of state dominion or jurisdiction over the church and his conscience. More died, not so much for any one historic pope – friend of Erasmus and of so many diplomats with Roman experience that he was, he could have had no illusions about Julius or Leo, or Clement VII, their dilatory successor, who helped the Reformation to come to a boil in England through his calculated strategy of doing nothing over Henry's divorce proceedings – or even for the general notion of the papacy. More's death resulted directly from his belief that no lay ruler could have jurisdiction over the church of Christ, and his concept of the church was more compatible with a post-Vatican II concept than with a Tridentine one' (R. J. Schoeck, 'Common Law and Canon Law' in Sylvester and Marc'hadour, *Essential Articles*, op. cit., 48). Schoeck fails to recognise that it is precisely the papacy that guarantees the independence of the local Church in opposition to the Erastian tendencies of the State. More, in his speech from the dock, clearly recognised this when he affirmed that 'no temporal prince [may] presume by law to take upon him, as rightfully belonging to the See of Rome, a spiritual preeminence by the mouth of our Saviour himself ...' (E. E. Reynolds, *The Trial of St Thomas More*, Wheathampstead, Herts, Anthony Clark Books, 1964, 121.)
51. By George M. Logan and Robert M. Adams in their introduction to *Utopia*, op. cit., xxiii
52. Ibid., xxiv.
53. cf *Utopia*, Book I, ibid., 20.
54. cf ibid., 37.

true nature had to be underlined, namely virtue, understood in the original Greek sense as 'excellence' (*areté*).

'The passage on moral philosophy', it has been remarked, 'is in fact the cornerstone of the Utopian edifice.'[55] Indeed, the rest of the account of the ideal commonwealth would seem to be primarily concerned with ideal conditions necessary for virtue to flourish: even one of the two games played by the Utopians was a battle of vices against the virtues.[56] Let us pay a little attention to the passage entitled 'Ethica' by the glossator.

To understand the nature of happiness – which as St Thomas Aquinas, following a tradition going back to Aristotle, affirms is the end of all virtue[57] – is almost impossible, the Utopians insist, without reference to two basic tenets of natural religion: the immortality of the soul and reward for virtue, punishment for vice in the hereafter.[58] Without an hereafter, there is no sense in en-

57. Evidently the more severe, not to say pessimistic, extreme Augustinian tradition was gaining, or rather had already gained, the upper hand at the time. It is of interest to note, in an aside, that it was Aquinas who placed the treatise on the Beatitudes at the very start of his discussion of virtue. There is no discussion of morality without first determining our final end, eternal happiness, union with God, eternal beatitudes. The new *Catechism of the Catholic Church* has restored it to that position after centuries of displacement that seems to have begun in the sixteenth century. More evidently saw the significance of such shifts in perspective

58. cf ibid., 68ff. The translation by G. C. Richards as revised by Surtz and Hexter (Yale edition) reads as follows: 'In that part of philosophy which deals with morals, they carry on the same debates as we do. They inquire into the good: of the soul and of the body and of the external gifts ... They discuss virtue and pleasure, but their principal and chief debate is in what thing or things, one or more, they are to hold that happiness consists. In this matter they seem to lean more than they should to the school that espouses pleasure as the object by which to define either the whole or the chief part of human happiness.

'What is more astonishing is that they seek a defence for this soft doctrine from their religion, which is serious and strict, almost solemn and hard. They never have a discussion of philosophy without uniting certain principles taken from religion as well as from philosophy, which uses rational arguments. Without these principles they think reason insufficient and weak by itself for the investigation of true happiness. The following are examples of these principles. The soul is immortal and by the goodness of God born for happiness. After this life rewards are appointed for our virtue and good deeds, punishment for our crimes. Though these principles belong to religion, yet they hold that reason leads men to believe and admit them.' (161, 17-163, 5).

during the hardship [*aspera*] that virtue necessarily involves. Behind this passage is one of the fundamental assumptions of medieval Catholic thought which seems to pervade every aspect of More's life and writings, namely the inter-relatedness of faith and reason; 'Reason is the servant of faith and not enemy.'[59] Under the influence of Nominalism, the Reformation was about to sunder one from the other radically – with enormous consequences, *inter alia*, for moral philosophy.[60]

The starting point is pleasure.[61] 'Now, indeed, [the Utopians] hold happiness rests not in every pleasure, but only in that which is good and upright. To such, as to the supreme good, our nature is drawn by virtue itself. The opposite school claims that virtue is itself happiness.'[62] The dispute between the Epicureans and Stoics behind these two views may be left aside, since More would seem to have transcended them by interpreting the Stoic concept of the *summum bonum*, in the light of Augustine's insight that we are made for God and are restless until we rest in him, and so recovering the original Aristotelian concept.[63] What More says is that in us there is an attraction to the ultimate Good, to the extent that we have achieved human excellence (virtue). This attraction is our capacity for happiness. As we will see, this attraction would seem to be the source of conscience.

'The Utopians define virtue as living according to nature since to this end we were created by God.'[64] This is a definition

59. Works, 1557, 152, as quoted in R.W. Chambers, op. cit., 253.
60. See Servais Pinckaers, *The Sources of Christian Ethics*, translated from the third edition by Sr Mary Thomas Nogle, OP (Edinburgh, 1995), 327-53; idem, *Morality. The Catholic View*, with a preface by Alasdair MacIntryre (South Bend, Indiana, 2001), 65-81.
61. We would do well to remember what Aristotle wrote: 'It is not possible to perform virtuous actions without pain or pleasure. The middle-state does not exist.' [no source given, quote found in *The Irish Catholic*].
62. *Nunc vero non in omni voluptate felicitatem sed in bona, atque honesta sitam putant. ad eam enim uelut ad summum bonum, naturam nostram ab ipsa pertrahi, cui sola aduersa factio felicitatem tribuit.* [Yale ed., 162, 15-18] The translation is my own.
63. 'The good is that to which all things aim' (Aristotle, *Nichomachean Ethics*, Bk I, Ch. 1. 104a 3, as given in Fagothy's *Right & Reason: Ethics in Theory and Practice*, ed Milton A. Gonsalves, Ninth Edition, [Columbus, Toronto, London, Melbourne, 1986], 67).
64. *Nempe uirtutem definiunt, secundum naturam uiuere ad id siquidem a deo institutos esse nos* [Yale ed., 162, 18-21], trs Surtz and Hexler.

of the Stoics, as the gloss observes, albeit transformed by Christian theology. We moderns have great difficulty understanding this statement, due to the prevailing false, moralistic view of virtue, as mentioned already. The Thomistic description, according to Josef Pieper, is 'the optimum that a human being can be', human flourishing at its best, as God intended we should flourish. The text continues:

> That individual, they say, is following the guidance of nature who, in desiring one thing and avoiding another, obeys the dictates of reason. Now reason first of all inflames [mortals] to a love and veneration of the divine majesty, to whom we owe both our existence and our capacity for happiness. Secondly, it admonishes and urges us to lead a life as free from care and as full of joy as possible, and because of our natural fellowship, to help all other men too, to attain that end.[65]

This is a most significant passage. It opens with the Thomistic concept of conscience: namely that right reason which, according to a recent commentary, 'enables men to distinguish right from wrong with instinctive clarity, that is to apprehend the natural law.'[66] I think that a further clarification is needed: More would have understood the term reason not in the abstract, rationalist sense familiar to us but in the classical sense of *logos*,

---

65. *Eum uero naturae ductum sequi quisquis in appetendis fugiendisque rebus obtemperat rationi. Rationem porro, mortales primum omnium in amorem, ac uenerationem diuinae maiestatis incendere, cui debemus, & quod sumus, & quod compotes esse felicitatis possumus, secundum id commonet, atque excitat nos ut uitam quamlicet minime anxiam, ac maxime laetam ducamus ipsi, caeterisque omnibus ad idem obtinendum adiutores nos pro naturae societate praebeamus.* [Yale ed., 162, 21-28], trs Surtz and Hexler.
66. Logan and Adams, op. cit., 69. Koterski, op. cit., p. xiii-xiv, assigns Thomas More a traditional Catholic understanding of conscience 'as a faculty by which an individual can pass moral judgments about the choices one intends to make as well as about choices already made. A well-formed conscience will evaluate these choices on the basis of moral truths that are antecedent to the will of the moral agent. In accord with the scholastic tradition that More knew from his days at Oxford, he took the formation of conscience to be the effect of a lengthy process of DISCOVERING the moral order and not a matter of DECIDING on what such an order was to be, for himself or for his age.'

reason perfected in the cognition of truth,[67] speculative and practical – in other words, wisdom – or the mind of the wise person which has come to recognise the intelligible order of being.

The order of human existence is the law. And that law, as More goes on to clarify in the next passage, is the dual commandment to love God and one's neighbour, since, as More comments: '[concern for, and action on behalf of, others] is the virtue most peculiar to man'.[68] His formulation of the natural law is, however, uniquely his own. First of all, reason (perfected in truth) inflames all mortals to a love and veneration of the divine majesty. More is not talking about a Deistic God infinitely distant from us but the transcendent God who is closer to each one than we are to ourselves. His use of the term 'inflames' is to be noted. Reason, secondly, warns us to live a joy-filled life free of care – this, it seems to me, is but another description of virtue – and to lead others to share that joy, namely love of God and a life free of all care and need, both material and spiritual. More underlines this with a lovely touch of irony ridiculing the long-faced proponents of virtue (the moral zealots of his day, and our day as well): if even they could understand that concern for the poverty and the sorry plight of others is humane and so to be fostered, then surely nature, presumed to be good, could be expected to urge everyone to do the same. The Catholic assumption that nature, though flawed, was basically good, was soon to be vehemently denied. The chill announcing the arrival of the storm brewing in Lower Saxony was already in the air. Is this the reason why More makes the Epicurean starting point his own in the discourse on moral philosophy we have just glanced at?

Behind this, the central text of *Utopia*, is what Ratzinger calls the ontological level of conscience, our capacity to know the truth both at the speculative and at the practical level. It is at this level, it seems to me, that we discover what moved More so pro-

---

67. Note, however, Josef Pieper's warning: 'We incline all too quickly to misunderstand Thomas Aquinas' words about reason perfected in the cognition of truth. "Reason" meant to him nothing other than "regard for and openness to reality" and "acceptance of reality". And "truth" is to him nothing other than the unveiling and revelation of reality, of both natural and supernatural reality.' (*The Four Cardinal Virtues* (Notre Dame, 1966), 9.

68. Surtz and Hexler use the term 'humanity' for what I have placed in brackets; so do Logan and Adams.

foundly, what moulded his life and death: the truth. Truth is ultimately incomprehensible but capable of some limited though
real comprehension, which is often discovered in the process of
trying to communicate it to others, as both poet and prophet testify. The truth, though always personal is not subjective. It is
communal and so universal. As Brodsky once said, reason is essentially social. Aristotle, I think, would have agreed, since he
used two definitions of man which, I suggest, are interchange-
able: a rational animal and a political animal. More died a witness to the truth (the definition of a martyr), and not simply for
his personal conviction. Truth is not individualistic. Though intensely personal and particular in its recognition and expression,
truth is by nature universal and communal. It is for this reason
that God instituted an ultimate, universal authority – the conscience of a particular person, the Successor of St Peter – to be
the guarantor of his revealed truth intended for the salvation of
all mankind. In More's own words, after he had studied the
question of Papal Supremacy, '… it holdeth up all'.[69] There is,
therefore, an intrinsic, and not just an accidental, relationship
between More's conscience and the papal supremacy, as he himself seems to have indicated when, after his judgement, it was
'prudent' for him to break his silence.[70]

Individuals may deny the truth, and indeed they may sincerely hold the opposite, in which case (erroneous conscience)
they are to be respected. According to the *Utopia*, they should be
tolerated, encouraged to debate the issue with the experts behind closed doors – and otherwise left to themselves in the hope
that one day they will see the truth and repent, as was the case
with Pico della Mirandola, the subject of More's first publication. What they cannot do, according to the *Utopia*, is speak
publicly about it, which would amount to imposing their views
on society and thus causing social unrest.[71] With regard to those
who do wrong, who act unjustly, like the judges who condemned More – God alone knoweth how, as he says – the only

---

69. Ibid., 196.
70. cf. R.W. Chambers, op. cit., 340. For the text of that speech, see E. E.
Reynolds, op. cit., 120f.
71. The threat to public order posed by heretical movements was fully
recognised by medieval society and was the justification for harsh measures against heretics by those who represented the State, such as
Thomas More as Lord Chancellor and so responsible for the common
good of the State.

thing one can do is pray that one day they too will, thanks to God's grace and mercy, acknowledge their wrongdoing and repent. Because More's own great matter was truth, or rather conscience understood as the primordial sensorium of truth, he could not only forgive his enemies but sincerely pray that those who condemned him would one day repent – and that they would finally recognise the truth so that they would all be merry together in heaven.[72] His merriment, I suggest, was likewise due to his passion for the truth, not his own convictions. He was literally 'care-free'. The truth had made him free.

---

72. 'Pray for me', More wrote to his daughter, Margaret, in his last letter from the Tower, 'and I shall for you and all your friends, that we may merrily meet in heaven' (*St Thomas More, Selected letters*, edited by E. F. Rogers [New Haven, 1961], 258).